Praise for
The MAINE THING

Through charming anecdotes, this book pulls the reader into deep reflection and nostalgic memories of small-town New England, providing a sense of confidence and comfort as one navigates the uncertainties of life.

> — Eric Army, AIA, CEO & Founder, Signal Works Architecture

Coming from the mental health profession, I encourage everyone to read this book... Elizabeth articulates struggles and experiences that so many face, myself included. Elizabeth connects her foundation of faith with readers who come from many different backgrounds. Her topics on identity, anxiety, and control really resonate with me, reminding me that my goal and calling is not myself, but others...and the One who created us.

> — Jordan Vance, DNP, FNP-BC, PMHNP-BC,
> Mental Health Professional

I have read many encouraging and motivational books but none better than this one. "It is more blessed to give than to receive," and Elizabeth has definitely given generously from her heart and life in this book.

— Herschel Hafford, Founder, President and Pastor
of I CARE Ministries, Millinocket, Maine.

This book is written with much love and appreciation for her many God-given experiences; even the difficult times uncover the positive new directions life can have.

— Anne Jackson

Take off your shoes and walk a garden path; you will feel the soft warm earth and the stones beneath your feet.

— Randy Jackson, Founder and President of the
Board at Boreal Theater, Millinocket, Maine

Reading this book feels like enjoying tea time with a dear friend; the words on the pages come alive with Godly wisdom, humor, and rich life stories that will encourage readers to live life in pursuit of God's unique and good purpose.

— Sarah Lavezzo, Founder and Executive
Director of Wonder Learning Collective

Elizabeth's stories of her youth, in a quaint and loving Maine community, are a beautiful reminder of how our past experiences shape who we are and how, if we are faithful, God continually nudges us forward on the path He has set for us.

— Jennifer Dorr, Associate Head Cross Country and
Distance Track Coach, Roberts Wesleyan University

The steadfast heart of the pioneer will be enlightened and grateful as it rediscovers the paths back to all that is good and true in life.

— Connilee Walter, Advisor & Advocate for Purpose-Driven Organizations and Individuals

I enjoyed reading about Elizabeth's journey and rediscovering herself and her purpose. I could imagine myself there in all the scenarios she described. It was a wonderful read and very encouraging. Loved the quotes and Scriptures before each chapter.

— Theresa Danzik, Entrepreneur

I'm motivated to rise above the noise in my life and focus on the enduring happiness that only meaningful relationships bring!

— Lynee Fife, Director, Children's Entrepreneur Market

This book reminds me that being a Godly woman doesn't mean constant love, light and peace, but that God equips me, sometimes through the miraculous, to always have victory over darkness.

— Stephanie Pierucci, CEO, Pierucci Publishing

A gentle reminder to inhale what moves me every day, not allowing busyness to deter me from quality time with my community, my family, and most importantly for myself and God.

— Chelsea Hover, Yoga Guide

This book illustrates to the reader that the only thing that is constant is change...Choose to hold God's hand and journey *through* the mountain, then all the hope and joy we carried with us as children will reappear as a soft light on the other side.

— Russell Womack, Author

This memoir clearly expresses how the smallest details in life seem to yield the greatest rewards in our lives.

— Laura Dobson, Co-Founder, Rebel Parenting

The Maine Thing really pulls you into many stories of the author's past and how it has greatly shaped the faith filled, resolute, accomplished, serving woman she has become. Elizabeth consistently reminds the reader that regardless of what you're experiencing, that God is in the details and meets us where we are.

— Julie Reed, Vice President of Customer Service, NDCP

In *The Maine Thing*, Elizabeth does a beautiful job of being vulnerable, tender, and authentic. When reading her stories, I was wrapped up in her storytelling and wisdom, spurring me on to deep self-reflection and joy.

- Katelyn Swiatek, The Fierce Women Podcast

Elizabeth's warm and inviting reflections about lessons learned from her unique experiences growing up in Maine with lobsters and bear hunting, inspire readers to take stock of the things in life that really matter and look back on their own treasure trove of formative memories.

- Wendy Gossett, M.Ed., Temperament Specialist

The MAINE THING

The MAINE THING

Rediscovering the way life should be

Elizabeth Reed Watkins

PIERUCCI PUBLISHING

THE MAINE THING

eBook ISBN 978-1-962578-23-3
Hardcover ISBN 978-1-962578-24-0
Paperback ISBN 978-1-962578-26-4

Design by Isaac Watkins
Author photo by Isaac Watkins
Edited by Teri Nott

Published by Pierucci Publishing
P.O. Box 2074, Carbondale, Colorado 81623, USA
www.pieruccipublishing.com

Library of Congress Control Number: 2024911812

Pierucci Publishing books may be purchased in bulk at special discounts for sales promotion, corporate gifts, fundraising, or educational purposes. Special editions can be created to specifications. For details, contact the Special Sales Department, Pierucci Publishing, PO Box 2074, Carbondale, CO 81623 or Publishing@ PierucciPublishing.com or toll-free telephone at 1-855-720-1111.

DEDICATION

This book is dedicated to my parents, Ken and Diane Reed. Dad and Mom, it's because of you that I have these stories to write about! Thank you for your courage and commitment. You persevere through life's ups and downs with faith, hope, and grace. Your example inspires me. Most of all, thank you for your love. You continue to believe in me and give me a place to belong. Mother Teresa once said, "If you want to change the world, go home and love your family." You've done this well, and your legacy will continue to live on. I love you so much. Thank you — for everything.

CONTENTS

INTRODUCTION

My spirit is overwhelmed within me;
My heart within me is distressed.

I remember the days of old;
I meditate on all your works.

— Psalm 143:4–5 (NKJV)

Let Him turn it in your favor,

Watch Him work it for your good,

He's not done with what He started,

He's not done until it's good.

— Maverick City Music*

In the Fall of 2022, shortly after my fortieth birthday, I entered into an emotionally chaotic, anxiety-riddled season of life. People who know me say that I am typically very optimistic, excited about life, goal-oriented, and driven. However, for weeks, which turned into months, and then more than a year, I lost my optimism. I lost my sense of direction. I had little drive for the day, and my once-clear goals were foggy. Although each new day dawned with a beautiful sunrise, I didn't see the beauty. I struggled in my pursuit of purpose and didn't know which goals to set for the future.

December dawned, but instead of feeling the joy of the Christmas season, I stood sobbing in the kitchen. When my husband asked what was wrong, I tried to communicate what I was feeling. "I am forty years old," I moaned. "What am I doing with my life? I feel no sense of purpose. I feel no direction. I haven't accomplished anything with my life, and I don't know what I am supposed to do moving forward! I wake up every morning feeling totally overwhelmed, and I don't like my life! How many days in a row can I wake up and not want to get up? Something has to change, but I don't know what!"

Have you ever been there? It's a difficult place.

Overwhelming feelings of hopelessness continued to plague me day after day. I felt overextended with work, misunderstood at home, and like I was failing in every area of life. My key priorities were my partnership with my incredible husband and parenting my four children. Yet each day, they were receiving "Elizabeth's leftovers." All of my other responsibilities ravenously consumed the best of what I had to offer. From the outside, my life may have looked pretty good. I had a fulfilling job as well as my own business. I was launching an entrepreneurial program for children. I lived in a beautiful home. Yet I felt totally lost and without purpose. The demands of my world were pulling me in multiple directions — too many directions.

In his book, *The Ruthless Elimination of Hurry*, John Mark Comer states,

"There is a healthy kind of busyness where your life is full of things that matter, not wasted on empty leisure or trivial pursuits...The problem isn't when you have a lot to do; it's when you have too much to do and the only way to keep the quota up is to hurry..."*

That was me. My pursuits were worthwhile, and I truly enjoyed each of my endeavors. Yet I was in "hurry mode" from the moment I woke up until the moment I went to bed, and I was not enjoying life anymore. When I tried to recall the last time I'd enjoyed my life, I was surprised to realize that it had been over a decade. If I allowed myself to stop long enough to ponder, questions screamed through my soul, causing great unrest. *Am I just a "human doing" or am I actually a "human being?" What is the difference between the two? What are my values, and am I living them out? Is there a greater purpose in life than the daily grind? Who am I? Why am I here?*

I am fairly confident I am not the only one who wrestles with these questions.

At that time, I was reading *Win the Day* by Mark Batterson. I'd just finished a chapter entitled "Postimagining," where Mark encourages readers to revisit their past and recognize their defining moments. It's a way to see the hand of God at work in your life, painting a beautiful masterpiece of creative artwork, one brush stroke at a time. Because I felt disconnected from the divine perspective of God's purpose for my life, I thought it would be a worthy exercise to complete. So, for the better half of December, I started journaling like I hadn't journaled in a long time. I started writing about significant relationships as well as those I still desired to cultivate; dreams fulfilled and dreams still held close to my heart; faith-filled moments and moments I was still living by faith. I wrote about jobs I'd had and businesses I'd started, and those I desired to start in the future. Moments I'd felt the most fulfilled and moments I'd felt the most lost....I wrote these in my journal. And that was how this book began.

As I reviewed my entries, I began to see God's hand at work in a most beautiful way. I noticed He was there throughout my journey. By looking back, I discovered His purpose for my life. It was greater than myself. I could also see that my life was beautiful — just because my Father in Heaven created me — that He loved and valued me. Deeply.

Then January 2023 rolled around. Within the first week of the New Year, my parents, my sister, Helene, and Helene's family visited my Colorado home. It was a lovely time of recalling old memories and creating new ones (so sorry for the broken arm, Mom!). We spent hours around the dinner table enjoying amazing food. We discussed answers to "dinner questions" my husband brought to the table each evening. For those of you who know the Reed family, you understand when I say there were lots of emotions. We shared laughter and tears liberally. It was a wonderful time of refreshment for all of us. Everyone left that week ready for the new year ahead. As we recounted past memories, we marveled at God's goodness and faithfulness.

Helene and I remembered little things from our childhood in Maine. We realized our previous "Maine years" helped shape our current values. Although we only lived there ten years, I've retained a collection of vivid memories from that time. It was a life so different from my current reality. In our modern world, those times were unlike anything that most people ever get to experience.

During that visit, I brought up an idea I'd been mulling over for several years. At one of our family dinners I asked, "What would you think if I wrote a book about our experiences in Maine?" The feedback was positive. My dad, especially, encouraged me to move forward with the idea. I later bounced the idea off of my husband, Isaac. He matter-of-factly said, "Just do it." But I doubted myself and laughed at his response. "Just do it?!" I countered. "What do you mean, 'just do it'? I've never written a book before. I don't know how to just do it." He challenged my mindset. As I pondered his words, I realized he had a point. *Okay,* I thought to myself, *I guess I will "just do it."* So, during the busiest season I'd ever experienced, I began to write. Now the book became more than journal entries. It had a purpose for others, too.

I wish I could say that my decision to write a book turned my despondency around immediately — that life began to make sense — it didn't. The New Year brought unanticipated challenges. Due to these unexpected circumstances, my heart and mind experienced upheaval and pain.

I couldn't make sense of all that was happening around me. Yet, as I wrote stories and Scriptures from my childhood, I found an anchor. I thought about those verses. I discovered God's never-ending goodness and His always-and-forever faithfulness showing up in my stories again and again. Those memories became faith monuments to my weary, nearly defeated soul. Thankfulness broke through the layers of hopelessness. I rediscovered the truth that, "Discouragement cannot live in a grateful heart."

Soon gratefulness started to take over. I added more stories to each chapter. And more and more gratitude flooded my heart and mind. Words began to tumble out of my spirit and onto the pages — memory upon memory, moment upon moment, miracle upon miracle. Whether I recounted hunting with my dad, serving with my mom, building friendships with my neighbors, or overcoming the obstacles of my adolescence, I often needed to pause while writing because grateful tears were running down my cheeks.

As I remembered treasured people and defining moments, I could see where I'd developed my values. As I outlined my values, my life story began to make sense. My purpose began to unfold. My identity began to take shape. Gratefulness and peace began to flood my heart. I started to find God again.

I realized what my Creator had known all along: I was fearfully and wonderfully made. God's plans for me were good plans; He was for me and not against me; no weapon fashioned against me would prosper. His angels surrounded me in all ways; no good thing did He withhold from me.

The song "It's Always Been You" by Phil Wickham ministered to my heart and mind during the season of writing:

"You are the voice that calms the storm inside me
Castle walls that stand around me
All this time, my guardian was You
You are the light that shines in every tunnel
There in the past, You'll be there tomorrow
All my life, Your love was breaking through

It's always been You
It's always been You"

As you read these stories, wandering through my memories and traveling my journey from overwhelm to peace, I hope you will remember and reflect on your own story. As you do, look for these load-lifting treasures on the way: God has uniquely fashioned you. You are created for community. You are deeply pursued and loved. Your past is significant, yet it doesn't have to define your future. You have a purpose that is greater than yourself.

And now, come see what life once looked like in a small town in a beautiful part of Maine, and how God showed up in the mess and in the beauty. May you feel empowered and excited to discover the treasure hidden in your own beautiful story, finding purpose, experiencing peace, and choosing gratitude along the way.

I have to warn you, when I looked back, it wasn't all good. At one point, I almost lost it all. Those were hard stories to share, but maybe some you can relate to as well. I had to dig through the difficult before I could find the gold.

The Ruthless Elimination of Hurry
*"Fear is Not My Future," by Maverick City Music

Rediscovering
COMMUNITY

For the whole Law (concerning human relationships) is fulfilled in one precept,

'You shall love your neighbor as yourself'

(that is you shall have an unselfish concern for others and do things for their benefit).

— Galatians 5:14 (AMP)

Neighborhoods are only neighborhoods
if we talk to one another.

Otherwise our homes are only
places where we sleep.

— Author Unknown

CHAPTER ONE

From the day we drove into Millinocket until the day we left, my family experienced community. Our neighbors welcomed us. Church members served us. Professionals cared for us. We immediately felt welcomed and valued by everyone in this small town.

Great Northern Paper established Millinocket in 1899. It's remotely located over 250 miles north of the Maine border. In its infancy, Millinocket grew so quickly that it earned the name "Magic City." Great Northern Paper expanded to be the largest paper mill in the world. During its prime, it generated 240 tons of paper per day. The mill employed the majority of Millinocket's population. If families didn't have employment at the mill, they were in the minority. Throughout the 20th century, Millinocket remained a thriving community. The town lived in a bubble of protection. Most Millinocket residents lived the American dream. Even during the challenges of the Great Depression, the people of Millinocket maintained their jobs. They supported their families. During the tail end of its prosperous years, my family moved to this quaint town.

Many aspects make Millinocket desirable. First, the town is conveniently located next to Baxter State Park. The forested park boasts Mt. Katahdin and the end of the Appalachian Trail. The area is also home to the renowned West Branch of the Penobscot River. Sportsmen from all over New England enjoy hiking and fishing around Millinocket. Additionally, the town maintains a modest population. It's a great place to raise a family. The remote location draws people who desire respite from modern-world distractions.

All of these attributes drew my family to Millinocket. In July of 1991, my family left New York State and moved to the remote wilderness of Maine. Dad had just stepped out of his culinary career and started his own taxidermy business. As is consistent with new businesses, he experienced financial strain. Then he received a call from his Millinocket friend, Bob Catalano. Bob encouraged him to venture north. Dad always enjoyed adventures, so he and Mom decided to relocate our family to Maine. I consider my parents modern-day pioneers.

When they decided to move, my parents had meager finances, no jobs, and few connections. They also had a family with five young kids. At eight years old, my twin sister, Laurel, and I were the oldest. My next sister, Helene, was four. Amber had just turned one. And my only brother, Seth, was just six months old. Despite their circumstances,

Dad and Mom embraced the opportunity. I am forever grateful for their decision. Growing up in Millinocket shaped me into who I am today.

The day we arrived, we came into town from the east. We drove slowly since the local speed limit was only 25 miles per hour. We passed through the town's only stoplight. All too quickly, we arrived at 95 Knox Street — our new home. The house sat one block from Millinocket's western boundary and only two blocks from the paper mill. The paper mill extended along the south end of town. Yet our house was only two short miles from the eastern entrance! As we pulled into the driveway, I was taken aback by the sight of our "new" home. I wasn't accustomed to finery, but even my eight-year-old mind understood this property needed a lot of work.

Built in 1930, the modest, two-story home stood abandoned and left to the elements. My younger siblings could have gotten lost in the overgrown grass. Weeds filled up the front yard. Laurel and I ventured toward the backyard. The lot was small, so our exploration didn't take long. A large rock sat off to the right. It offered a natural barrier between the neighbor's garage and our property. Beyond the rock, a split rail fence divided the neighbor's yard from ours. Old wire fencing stood between our property and the house behind us. To my left a vertical board fence blocked any view of the other yard. A myriad of trees offered shade at random points along the property line. As Laurel and I wandered around, glass crunched under our feet. We later discovered the previous owners held lots of parties. Their guests liked to throw glass bottles at the rock. Most of the shattered remnants remained.

Without much luck in the backyard, I hoped the inside of the house might offer more promise. Laurel and I hiked back to the front. We walked up the cracked, brick steps and through the enclosed front porch. From there we entered the kitchen. To this day I can still remember my disbelief as I looked up at the ceiling. The sheetrock had suffered water damage and caved in. The exposed ceiling revealed water and heating pipes. Debris scattered all over the floor.

The sights didn't improve in the living room. When new, the living room must have welcomed visitors with its calming, robin-egg blue carpet. However, by the time we arrived, the carpet was worn out and filthy. Cigarette butts, dirt, and dust turned any remaining blue into a grimy gray. That carpet stopped at the stairs where bright orange carpet took over, traveling up the stairs and into three tiny bed-rooms. Maybe the previous owners felt adventurous after one of their parties and decided to add additional color to their lives! All the other ceilings were intact. Yet every single window in the home was broken. In fact, everything needed complete attention. Amazingly, my mother didn't complain. She looked around and quietly thanked my dad for providing the home.

My optimistic father had a vision for what the home could become. He helped my mom visualize the finished product. Over the next several months, my parents would bring Dad's vision to life. But there were a lot of adventures between pulling into that driveway and moving into the house.

From the day we saw that house, the Millinocket community gathered around us. They welcomed us and provided us with much-needed assistance and connections. We began to experience what makes a true community. It all began with the people of Millinocket Church of the Nazarene.

Pastored by my dad's friend, Bob Catalano, the small church acted as the hands and feet of Jesus. Pastor Bob inspired Dad to move to Maine. My parents arrived with a young family. But they also were without livable housing, jobs, and other necessities. Pastor Bob encouraged his church to help us in any way that was needed. And they did.

When we arrived, we couldn't live in the house. So one of the church members offered a temporary solution. The church member's name was Dr. Larry. Dr. Larry owned the local chiropractic office and lived in town. He also maintained a camp at a nearby lake.

In Maine, a "camp" is like a rustic cabin. If you've ever seen the television show, The Maine Cabin Masters, you'll have an idea of what they look like. Unrenovated camps have walls, windows, doors, and a roof to provide essential shelter from the weather. Stocked with beds, fishing gear, and equipment for water fun, they are places to let loose and enjoy the simple life of being outdoors. At that time, many were still without running water, electricity, and indoor plumbing. These wooden "tents" dotted the shores of the many lakes surrounding Millinocket.

The lakes in the area are beautiful! North Twin Lake and South Twin Lake sparkle to the west. Ambejejus Lake and Millinocket Lake beckon from the north. Dr. Larry's camp sat on a secluded piece of South Twin Lake shoreline.

My father and mother accepted Dr. Larry's invitation, and our adventure continued.

Dr. Larry's camp was six miles outside of town. Remotely located at the end of a dirt road, the camp offered two small rooms, including a kitchen and a bedroom. Yet it did not have running water. The camp's modest two rooms were indeed cramped for our large family. The lack of running water added another dimension to daily life. Even so, we all remember that time with fondness. It was like going back in time to live like the pioneers.

My twin sister and I idolized the lifestyle of Mary and Laura Ingalls. We loved the adventures of *Little House on the Prairie*! We frequently pretended we were Mary and Laura and acted out our favorite adventures. After moving into Dr. Larry's camp, we felt excited to live a life similar to the Ingalls family!

Since modern conveniences weren't available at the camp, we added multiple tasks to our typical routine. We collected water from the natural spring on Turkey Tail Road. Far from the reverse osmosis bottled water of today, this water source trickled down a hillside. A strategically placed pipe allowed people access to the water. It was so cold and clean! Many South Twin Lake residents got their water from the spring. We drove to the spring every couple of days, scrambled down the embankment and refilled our empty milk jugs with fresh spring water. We collected enough to satisfy our needs for several days. Then we'd repeat the routine.

When we needed baths, we enjoyed the refreshing water of South Twin Lake. The water was clear and cold even during the summer months. Bath time at the lake was not relaxing or comfortable! As the weather started to change into the cooler temperatures of fall, Mom was the only one brave enough to continue outdoor baths. The rest of us waited until we could enjoy a warm shower in town!

Despite the challenges of living at the camp, we overflowed with thankfulness. We felt so loved by this new community. A complete stranger offered us his property! Ladies from the church cared for us kids while Mom worked on the house. The ladies also pitched in and helped her remodel.

Two women became very special during our transition time. They were the pastor's wife, Melanie Catalano, and church attendee, Debbi Perkins. Their families became dear friends. They gently offered their interior decorating skills and extra materials, such as wallpaper and paint. Together, they painted walls and restored the kitchen's pine cabinets and trim. Everyone worked together to make our house a home. The deteriorated kitchen transformed into a welcoming gathering place. Original spruce floors gleamed, replacing the awful robin-egg blue carpet. New windows sparkled. The front yard jungle vanished and backyard glass shards disappeared. The church community welcomed and surrounded us. They delivered meals as Mom and Dad worked from sunup to sundown. We experienced Millinocket's unique community during our first year in Maine.

There were several occasions when Laurel and I felt so cared for by these new friends. For the majority of our elementary and middle school years, Mom homeschooled us. But due to Mom's other responsibilities that first year, Laurel and I attended public school. Katahdin Elementary School was less than one mile away from our new home. It provided a great educational experience. The new opportunity excited us! But we also felt very unprepared. Since we were homeschooled, we weren't familiar with the annual back-to-school practices.

Caring to her core, Millinocket native and fellow church member, Debbi Perkins, joyfully embraced the opportunity to serve our family. She volunteered to take Laurel and me shopping. She purchased our backpacks, notebooks, and pencils. She picked out new sneakers, clothing, and pencil boxes. These items seemed extravagant since we didn't routinely practice back-to-school shopping. Debbi's kindness and hospitality accurately portrayed the beautiful people who surrounded us.

After the school year started, my parents drove Laurel and me from Dr. Larry's camp to our bus stop on Route 11 every day. Turkey Tail Road is a dirt road. The three-mile route from our cabin to the bus was a slow drive. We diligently planned a margin into each morning to make sure we arrived on time. The bus didn't wait for late children.

One cool September morning, Mom's car didn't start. Dad was already gone for the day. So we thought through other ways to get to the bus stop. Laurel and I convinced Mom to allow us to walk. She gave us specific instructions to return home if we did not arrive in time for the bus. We respectfully agreed and excitedly began our adventure. We safely arrived at the bus stop and patiently waited for the bus. However, we soon realized we missed the bus.

Laurel and I started rationalizing solutions other than returning home. From the time we were young, we embraced responsibility. Plus, we were always up for a challenge. Not intending to defy Mom's instructions, we decided to do the responsible thing and hike to school! We strapped our blue and pink backpacks onto our little shoulders. Then we began the trek toward town. We knew our plan might take some time. We just didn't realize how much time — or that town was six miles away.

We hadn't gone very far when an old sedan pulled alongside us. A middle-aged couple, who we later discovered lived just down the road from our camp, asked about our journey. "Where are you going?" they inquired. "We're walking to school!" we announced. We told them about our situation and our decision. The couple empathized with us. "Do you realize that town is six miles away?" they asked. We shook our heads. "Can we take you back home?" they wondered. "No," we told them. "We want to go to school." We assured them we were okay. Yet they were not okay leaving us there. They continued to gently admonish us to accept a ride, either back home or to school. Laurel and I knew we shouldn't ever take rides from strangers. "We are not going to leave you on the side of the road," they declared. So we gave in. And the couple dropped us off at school, safe and sound.

These were the kind of people who lived in Millinocket. They continually cared about and looked out for one another. I don't condone my childish actions. I had no idea what could have happened. In fact, when our teacher discovered the situation, she immediately notified our parents. Once home, Laurel and I received firm instructions against taking rides from strangers. However, I do think the experience further shaped me in a good way. Growing up in a town where people cared for one another developed a deep-seated trust in humanity. People cared for me. So I grew up trusting people. I still live my life believing most people are trustworthy.

As the years went on, I experienced more examples of this caring community. Throughout our years in Maine, Mom worked per diem as a nurse at Millinocket Regional Hospital. It was only two blocks from our home. The small hospital provided Mom with many connections. Because she only worked part-time and Dad's business was just getting established, my family had multiple years when we went without adequate health insurance. Even so, Mom scheduled the family's annual physicals and dental visits.

One of Millinocket's family medical providers was especially gentle and kind. He operated out of concern and care for his patients. When he discovered our family's situation, he charged my mom only $5 per child for our visits. (Out of respect for his acts of generosity, he will remain anonymous.) I will always remember the kindness he showed our family and his thoughtful goodwill.

Millinocket had great community spirit! The town celebrated and supported the youth. This support made a big impression on me. Throughout the years, the Stearns High School football team won multiple state championships. State achievement banners covered the walls of the high school gym. They boasted the students' commitment to achievement.

Friday home games drew an energetic crowd. The town eagerly supported high school athletes. At each home game, the high school pep band performed upbeat tunes. Laurel and I played in the pep band. The music added to the festive atmosphere. Players and attendees displayed school spirit.

Maine's fall season can be cold and dark. Despite the conditions, Friday football games provided Millinocket locals with opportunities to connect with friends and family. People who went to the games also generously supported fundraising activities. High school students frequently conducted bake sales. We offered homemade treats such as chocolate chip cookies, brownies, and a Maine favorite — whoopie pies! As a student, I felt so proud to be part of an honored high school culture.

In the spring, prom celebrated the turn of the season and brought everyone together! Stearns High School juniors hosted this event, and teachers allowed students' creativity to shine! Their support made us realize that even though our student body was small, we were capable of great things. The gym transformed into a glorious display of romantic beauty and fun.

Prom evening started with a "Grand March." Anyone could attend this event. And most everyone did. Imagine a high school rendition of a red-carpet event, and you will comprehend the evening. Attendees sat on the gym bleachers and eagerly waited. The DJ called the names of each couple. Couples entered the gym one by one and paraded before the town's audience. Attendees "Oohed" and "Awed" at the elegantly dressed young women and men. Parents and teachers praised the decorations and displays. Attendees left after the final couple's announcement. It was a beautiful procession. And the community support made students feel confident.

I didn't fully appreciate the camaraderie of our town during my years in Millinocket. However, I now stand amazed at the support and pride for the town's youth.

Over the years, Millinocket stayed the same in some ways and significantly changed in others. It started as a thriving community. It hummed with activity from the paper mill's prosperity. It offered residents a bright and stable future. Yet, between 1990–2008, the paper mill experienced multiple ownership changes. Partnered with the rise of technology and the decreased need for manpower, the mill's stability and profitability declined.

Unfortunately, due to bankruptcy, the mill closed its doors in 2008. As a result, many businesses and residents also closed their doors. They moved on to other communities. Today, Millinocket is a quiet town. It maintains a rhythm of seasonal tourism. Even so, community remains a core value. The many locals who remain are determined to create destiny out of destitution. And many are succeeding. One of those successes is the Millinocket Half-Marathon and Marathon.

Started in 2015 by runners from southern Maine, this race now supports over 1,000 runners each year. Runners come from all over New England to participate. It began as a humble initiative to generate commerce and support for Millinocket after the devastating mill closure. Since its inception, the race has generated over 3 million dollars. Every cent goes back into Millinocket's economy! The founders ask no entry fee. Instead all participants generously support local businesses. I look forward to running this race in the future, supporting the town that for so many years supported me.

Then there are my former neighbors, Randy and Anne Jackson. They wanted to reestablish Millinocket's downtown vibrancy. They also recognized the need for a cultural outlet in rural Maine. Their solution? Boreal Theater. This non-profit organization develops community through the visual and performing arts.

Randy and Anne initiated the vision. Yet the local and statewide arts community collaborated with them until their vision materialized. Boreal Theater's doors opened in 2022. Today, it serves Millinocket and the surrounding towns by celebrating local talent. It offers rural Maine residents and visitors opportunities for connection through a creative, cultural outlet.

Millinocket still undergirds and supports its youth in many ways. After the mill shut down, the town experienced extreme financial challenges. Multiple youth programs threatened to close. However, many Millinocket residents stepped up and met the needs around them. They explored alternative funding options. Several projects and people are worth mentioning. Our family friend, Debbi Perkins, and my classmates, Chris and Jessica McDonald, are some of these people.

Debbi started her first year as Stearns High School junior advisor in 2003. Debbi's daughter was a junior that year. Debbi assumed the role so she could assist with her daughter's class prom. It was also the first year the mill completely shut down. The town initially wanted to discontinue the prom. Yet Debbi decided to keep it going. She believed Stearns' students should still experience their long-anticipated event. So Debbi collaborated with organizations and businesses throughout Maine. Her efforts provided dresses, tuxedos, and other resources. The benevolent initiative succeeded and positively impacted other towns as well. Today, multiple statewide organizations continue this effort and provide prom resources for rural areas.

My former classmate, Chris McDonald, is also helping Millinocket's youth succeed. Laurel and I reconnected with Chris while visiting Millinocket in June 2023. At that time, his computer rehab shop occupied a place on Main Street. We dropped in to say "Hello." Chris warmly welcomed us. Through our brief conversation, Chris informed us that he and his cheerful wife, Jessica, returned to Millinocket in 2011. They discovered the local sports programs were in danger of closing. Lack of funding and lack of participation led to a decline in morale. Only a thin thread of hope kept the programs afloat.

Sports positively impacted Chris and Jessica throughout their youth. So they decided to do what they could to keep the programs going. Initially, they volunteered and collaborated with the established programs. Then they intentionally rebuilt sports morale. They did this by starting a "Meet the Athletes" day. Chris and Jessica opened their home. They invited elementary children to connect with high school athletes. Their efforts were a labor of love. Having three kids of their own, the McDonalds recognized the value of continuing to invest in the next generation.

Later on, Chris networked with former NFL players. He received funding to produce high-caliber football camps for up-and-coming athletes. Chris's involvement grew until he reestablished many aspects of Millinocket's well-known sports program. Excitement for Millinocket's youth re-ignited. Once again, Friday night football games are well-attended and celebrated.

I admire all of these wonderful efforts to rebuild a thriving community. Aren't these stories such beautiful examples of people coming together? Don't these stories inspire you to search out creative ways to pay it forward in your community? They do for me.

Growing up in a community-centric town impacted my heart deeply. Even though I cultivated few friendships while growing up, I loved connection. I experienced rich relationships. People prioritized each other. Neighbors knew one another. Medical professionals cared for their patients. Locals celebrated youth. The youth rose to the level of their expectations. All of these things greatly impacted my approach to life.

Today, cultivating connection is one of my greatest priorities. I pursue activities where community is valued. My relationships are more important to me than any material possessions. As I reviewed old journals and photo albums in preparation for this book, I found a clipping in one of my high school albums. It said, "Neighborhoods are only neighborhoods if we talk to one another. Otherwise, our homes are only places where we sleep." This statement touches my heart deeply.

Do you remember the 2020 epidemic of COVID-19? It was only a few short years ago as of writing this novel. The virus swept rapidly across the entire world. Yet isolation and loneliness seemed greater than the virus itself. Communities fractured. Families separated. Youth suffered. Since then, gatherings resumed. However, I still see the devastating effects of separation and loneliness. Despite prolific social media connections, people seem to be more isolated than ever before. What I see concerns me. It leaves me wondering how to cultivate connections on my street, neighborhood, town, and state.

I no longer live in a quaint town but in the booming metropolis of Colorado Springs. The Front Range boasts over three million people — three times the population of Maine! And thousands more are being added to that number every month. In some ways, it can be easy to get lost in the shuffle. Hundreds of thousands of people scurry around. Most are busily distracted in their own little worlds. Maybe you know what that's like.

I do.

For our first 15 years in Colorado, my husband and I lived in downtown Colorado Springs. Contrary to what you may think, our historic neighborhood maintained close-knit relationships. Block parties drew families out of their homes. On-street parking allowed neighbors natural interaction with one another. Neighborhoods celebrated kids by hosting child-led holiday parades. It was a lovely time in our lives. I wholeheartedly enjoyed our many years there.

In time, the downtown area no longer suited our needs. Circumstances abruptly moved our growing family outside the city's limits. We exchanged our quaint bungalow for a sprawling ranch-style home. We now enjoy mountain views and a big backyard.

Logically, this seemed like a good move. So why did I initially dislike our new location?

It dawned on me that I no longer felt known. My new neighbors quietly disappeared into their automatically maneuvered garages. The garages are conveniently attached to their homes. Times of connection occurred organically in our previous neighborhood. Now they were few and far between. Despite the beauty all around us, not as many people were out during the day. It took more effort to know our new neighbors.

When the isolation of COVID-19 hit, we really felt the lack of connection. We had lived in the neighborhood for almost two years, and yet we still hadn't met everyone on our street. We challenged ourselves to get out of the house. And we started connecting. We invited neighbors over for tea. We initiated neighborhood yard projects. We hosted barbecues. Not everyone accepted our invitations, but many did. Soon our cul-de-sac transformed. We now feel connected and known. All it took was a little extra intentionality.

Like me, do you desire additional community and connection? Does your life feel isolated and alone? Most likely those around you feel the same way. Try what we did. Start small. Step out of your home and walk across the street. Interact with your neighbors. Say hello. Invite people in for tea. Work together on a project outside. Host a barbecue! As you plant seeds of connection, community will begin to grow. Sometimes you may have a vision larger than you can accomplish on your own. Could you collaborate with others? People are often willing and excited to participate in a joint mission. Especially if that mission fosters community. Randy and Anne Jackson discovered this.

Could you also look for ways to support children? I believe people grow into what's expected of them. I think kids are the same. When you communicate your belief in their future, kids will rise to the level of your expectations. Didn't you?

In my current roles, I see evidence of this every day. Kids are capable of great things! Often, they just need a community to surround them. To believe in them. To undergird their pursuits. I admire the efforts of Debbi Perkins and Chris and Jessica McDonald. Their investments in Millinocket's youth will have a ripple effect for years to come.

I realize these simple suggestions won't change communities overnight. Yet I do believe solutions are simple. Little by little, a community revolution can begin with small steps in the right direction.

---

http://www.millinocket.org

Rediscovering
PURPOSE

Whatever you do in word or deed,
do all in the name of the Lord Jesus,
giving thanks through Him to God the Father.

— Colossians 3:17 (NASB1995)

The whole world, with one small
exception, is composed of others.

— John Maxwell

CHAPTER TWO

An entrepreneur and sportsman, Dad owned a fly shop, taxidermy studio, and guiding business. This meant summer and fall were especially busy. He took dozens of people hunting and fishing. He outfitted them before and preserved their memories after. Dad's businesses were the family's livelihood. We pitched in as a family to help Dad in any way we could. We served together. We all worked on different tasks and thoroughly enjoyed helping him. Bear season was my personal favorite.

Bear season started the last week of August and continued until mid-September. Hunters from all over New England ventured north with the desire to harvest a bear. In Maine, most sportsmen hunt bears using a tree stand. Bear hunters and guides set up "baits" to lure bears to their hunting area. Baiting bears takes skill and involves a lot of hard work.

Black bears are fascinating creatures. Their senses are quite different from ours. They have a sharp sense of vision — but only up close. Their hearing, twice the sensitivity of humans, is their first line of defense. They can hear in every direction. And their olfactory sense is truly magnificent. Their sense of smell is *one hundred times* that of humans! When baits are constructed properly, hunters can use this highly-tuned sense of smell to their advantage. But first, they have to find them.

Although bear season occurs during the early fall, preparations begin months in advance. Throughout the spring, Dad scouted the woods for signs of bears and established dozens of potential sites for his hunters. I am not sure how Dad knew where to look. His sites were remote, far from any civilization. He got permission from the state to access the dense forests surrounding logging roads. Many of these roads were dirt. Then he used old, overgrown paths that disappeared into the woods to reach the sites.

After finding hunting locations, Dad meticulously started his baits. First, he placed a "stink bait" made of pungent foods such as fish. If a bear discovered the bait, Dad deemed the bait successful. He restocked the bait with "goodies" every 7–10 days. Dad obtained these tasty treats from a variety of sources. He creatively networked to collect food. Local convenience stores donated their outdated goods. Previous culinary connections set aside their leftovers. Dad's out-of-state friends even helped. One summer, his dear friends, Bill Post and Dale Price, hauled a trailer load of baked goods from New York to Maine. They stopped long enough to rest with us for two hours before making the twelve-hour trip back to New York. So many people helped Dad with his efforts.

Remember that small backyard? Well it soon became the "Bear Bait Bucket Zone." Fifty-gallon drums collected the outdated baked goods. These goodies were then divided into five-gallon buckets which Dad transported to his hunting sites. He emptied their contents at his baits and brought the buckets back to the house for refills. He had dozens of baits, so this process was repeated over and over throughout the entire summer.

Throughout the summer months, it was our job as kids to prepare those five-gallon buckets. This was so much fun! While we filled the buckets, we sampled the barely-expired treats. Miniature apple pies and cherry turnovers were my favorites. I can still remember opening the wrappers, biting into the flaky crust, and savoring the sweetness! Doughnuts were my second choice. Everything was so delicious!

Sometimes we accompanied Dad to his sites. These trips often occurred spontaneously. All spring and summer, Dad worked so hard. He frequently left before dawn and didn't return until after dark. But occasionally he came home in the middle of the day. If we were around, he invited several of us to join him for the afternoon. We excitedly accepted because trips with Dad were always an adventure. Dad lived out of his truck during the summer. To find a place to sit, we cleared away coffee cups, flannel shirts, and candy wrappers. Dad's truck maintained a woodsy smell of earth, coffee, and sweat. Although his vehicles were usually older, I always felt safe driving around with Dad. I treasured this extra time with him.

When bear season finally arrived at the end of August, the warm summer weather transitioned. Brisk autumn temperatures changed the green forests into a fiery landscape. A hurried pace filled the air. Birds flew south. Animals scurried around, preparing for the relentless winter. We felt the same flurry of activity. We readied our hands, hearts, and home for the arrival of our hunter guests.

There were so many things to do before the hunters arrived. Mom organized and oversaw the deep cleaning of the house. We scrubbed every nook and cranny until it shone. Then our New York friends, Dale Price and Harold and Judy Coons, joined us. They served alongside Mom every year and cooked for the many guests.

During bear season, every Saturday was cooking day. We picked vegetables from the garden. We shucked fresh corn. We shredded cabbage and carrots for coleslaw. We peeled potatoes for potato salad. We prepared berries for pies. We baked loaves of bread and dozens of cookies. Smells of fresh goodies constantly filled the air. I did not have a consistent task but jumped in wherever I saw a need. We all worked together to generate enough food for our soon-arriving guests. It was a delightful time of laughter and fun.

My sister, Helene, always made the potato salad. She joyfully took charge of her responsibility, using our Nana Reed's special recipe. Helene diced potatoes. She hard-boiled eggs, and then she minced onions. Helene drizzled all the ingredients with olive oil, sprinkled with paprika, and added other seasonings until the mixture tasted just right. To this day, Helene is the potato salad expert!

My favorite dish to make was "Blueberry Diane." Affectionately named after my mom, the dessert was a mouthwatering combination of freshly picked Maine blueberries and a crunchy crumble topping. Sometimes we served it with ice cream or whipped cream. But most of the time, the hunters simply devoured it plain.

Each group of hunters arrived on Sunday afternoon. They stayed until the following Saturday. When Sunday rolled around, our house and our family were as ready as we could be. My siblings and I eagerly peeked out the front windows, waiting for the hunters to arrive. Pickup trucks and SUVs parked helter-skelter along each side of our small home. They pulled in wherever there was room. Once our guests unloaded, Dad welcomed them into our backyard. He gave a brief orientation of the week's schedule, accommodations, and expectations. Then the fun began!

To give hunters the full Maine experience, we started the week with a festive lobster feed. Even though we lived in the lobster capital of the Northeast, our family's lobster boils only occurred during bear season. So these feasts were a treat for all of us!

The cold Atlantic coastline produces an abundant supply of lobster. Maine is known for this delicacy. During the summer months, some fishermen from southern Maine make trips to Millinocket to sell fresh lobster. One of the fishermen was named Fred. Dad and Fred had an amicable relationship. Dad notified him weekly of his hunters' needs. Then Fred efficiently delivered Dad's request every Saturday. They met at "Peddler's Hill." This nondescript gravel parking lot gave vendors an outdoor marketplace to sell their products. It's still centrally located on Route 11, only one mile from our Knox Street home.

As hunters visited outside, Dad's assistant, Dale, took his place in the kitchen. At that time, we had a commercial-sized gas stove. On Sundays during bear season, it received constant attention. As Dale began his magic, twenty-quart lobster pots produced billows of steam. We served the steaming lobsters promptly — along with plenty of napkins! Removing the succulent meat from its shell is a tedious process. Yet all the hard work is immediately worth it. We dipped the meat into melted butter and placed the pieces in our mouths. We savored each juicy flavor before our next bite. We served all the other foods alongside the lobster. Everyone ate until satisfied. The feast was incredible! To this day, hunters still talk about our lobster bakes. And that was just the first day!

The real work began on Monday. Although still children at the time, we pitched in every day to prepare food. Lunch was the largest meal of the day and required a lot of preparation. Hunters shuttled into the woods before dawn. Yet they took a break at noon and traveled back to our home for lunch. Excitement filled the air as men boisterously shared their stories. They eagerly anticipated their afternoon in the forest.

My sisters and I happily served them. We refilled water glasses. We offered second and third helpings of stew, baked ziti, or pot roast. We passed out cookies and pie. We served coffee and tea. My heart overflowed with joy. I had a purpose greater than myself. I remember feeling fulfilled as I worked to meet the needs of those around me.

After the men departed for their afternoon hunt, we jumped into cleaning the disorder that was left behind. It was tedious work. We washed and dried loads of plates, glasses, pots, and pans. At that time, we didn't have a dishwasher. So we completed this task by hand. However, there was great pleasure and delight because we knew our work helped Dad with his business.

Following cleanup, we enjoyed an hour or two of quiet. We read, played outdoors, or sipped on cups of tea. However, the leisurely time came to an end all too quickly. Then the flurry of activity started again as we prepared for the hunters' return.

Days are shorter in autumn, so hunters maximize the daylight. Our hunters did not return to our home until close to bedtime. Mom served the evening meal around 7:30 p.m. or 8:00 p.m. — sometimes even later if hunts were successful. Evenings were my favorite! Hunters gathered around the table once again. The cuisine wasn't as elaborate as lunchtime. Sandwiches, soup, and cookies were common. Yet, the environment was even more animated than before! As hunters swapped their accounts, their excitement multiplied. Boisterous laughter accompanied their tales. Their stories grew larger and more animated as the evening wore on.

As kids, we rarely enjoyed the evening in its entirety. Disciplined to her core, Mom still strictly enforced our 8:30 p.m. bedtime. However, our bedrooms sat at the top of the staircase, and this allowed us to hear the men's stories.

Many nights I fell asleep listening to the comforting rumble of voices. It was a truly memorable time of year.

The weeks of service shaped me into the individual I am today. I continue to find joy in meeting the needs of those around me. Hosting others in my home is one of my favorite hobbies. I love welcoming a neighbor for a cup of tea, preparing dinner for a group of friends, or hosting guests for an extended stay. I feel the most purpose and fulfillment when serving. Contentment multiplies as I use my hands and home to provide a peaceful place for others.

One of my favorite books is *Generosity Factor: The Joy of Giving Your Time, Talent, and Treasure*. In this impactful short story, Ken Blanchard and S. Truett Cathy remind readers of the multiple ways we can serve. Our time, talent, touch, and treasure are gifts we give to others. As Blanchard and Cathy point out, serving is giving. I believe God has given each of us different strengths that can be used to minister to others. Those days of helping Dad in his business were ways of serving the physical needs of others around me. Perhaps this is why meeting people's immediate physical needs comes naturally to me. Blanchard and Cathy equate this to giving time. However, I am still learning how to serve others by extending a listening ear, embracing others with warmth, and giving finances toward needs in my community. I desire to slow down and invest my life in people. I tend to get busy taking care of physical needs and forget to stop and listen to those around me.

My mom is one of the greatest servers I know. She eagerly attends to the needs of everyone around her. Mom and I frequently chat about the joys — and inconveniences

— of serving. I've observed her grow and develop additional skills over the years. Currently, she's more interested in connecting with people in her home than in cultivating the space around them. Mom gently reminds me that guests come to see me and my family, not my home or what I can "do" for them. This reminder serves me well, especially in this busy season of raising a family.

My second favorite book on serving is called *Go-Givers Sell More*. Contrary to the title, the book focuses on serving. Authors Bob Burg and John David Mann challenge readers to change their mindset about success. Like my mom, they encourage people to focus on adding value to others. They suggest the most valuable gift to offer others is the gift of yourself. And be *present*.

I love people. Yet I am also an introvert. Sometimes I can be self-focused and introspective. Serving takes me out of my inner focus and turns my attention to the needs of people around me. I challenge myself daily to find some-one to serve. Sometimes it's as small as texting a word of encouragement to a friend or smiling at a stranger in the grocery store. Other times, it's more time-consuming such as helping a neighbor with a task.

I'm constantly rediscovering the inexplicable joy that comes when I focus on others. Serving the hunters and my dad was fun! Serving others with a smile or words of encouragement always lifts my spirits, too.

Since service impacted my life so greatly, I desire to cultivate this value in my children. A mentor of mine says, "Kids don't always do what you say, but they always do what you do." Isn't that the truth?! Mom's example certainly taught me to serve! She modeled a lifestyle of generosity. Now I'm inspired to look for ways that my family can be a giving family.

I recently heard about a 2023 report from the Surgeon General calling loneliness and isolation an epidemic in America that profoundly affects our health and well-being. When I remember bear season, I remember being a team. We weren't lonely at all. We worked alongside neighbors and friends and each other. Dad always attributed much of his success to the service of family and friends. Friends collaborated to make the entire season a success.

I find myself wondering how I can do something like that in my life today. We certainly don't run a guiding business or prep bait for bear season! But those memories were such fun, even in the hard work, that I am constantly looking for ways to connect my kids and our friends — pitching in so we're all a part of something bigger than ourselves.

Children these days are busier than ever, mine included. They're hustled to multiple sports and activities as soon as they can walk. And the busyness continues throughout their childhood and into their adolescent years. We were certainly busy but the busyness kept us connected.

As a parent of four children who will soon be entering their adolescent years, I wonder how I can help my kids combat this epidemic of loneliness. I feel the constant pressure and tension of involving them in different activities. If they aren't proficient in music, athletics, and other hobbies, will they still become successful contributors to society? I know the activities in and of themselves are beneficial. As a teen, I enjoyed music, horsemanship, and athletics.

But since thinking back to those days of serving with my family, which had such a profound impact on my life, I'm starting to wonder if giving my children opportunities to serve would equally cultivate their skills and self-worth. It certainly worked for me. Maybe delivering cookies to an elderly neighbor could be just as essential to my kids' growth as teaching them how to effectively play an instrument. And will I choose to serve with joy, even when I'm physically and mentally spent, like my mom served all of us? It's certainly given me a lot to think about.

Those are my wonderings. I have no answers yet, but looking back is helping me see that those times of working together as a family to serve others had a lot more benefits than just the work. It brought joy. I felt I had a purpose — my work mattered. And it gave us a sense of connectedness. It's been easy to lose that clarity along the journey of my life. I'm glad to be pondering it again and asking how I can create moments like that for myself and my family.

What about you? What is your mindset toward serving and giving? Did your parents or guardians model a servant's heart? If so, thank them! Not everyone had positive role models in this area. My friends who have challenges with serving have mentioned their lack of examples. They didn't practice serving as kids. I have another friend whose parents valued independence over serving. Now as an adult, thinking of others doesn't come as naturally to him.

For those of you who consistently serve, have you found that meeting others' needs produces joy and fulfillment? Do you seek out opportunities to care for people's physical, emotional, and financial needs?

I hope to encourage you to keep your eyes open to the needs around you. Your strengths and abilities may be different from mine. Your daily rhythm is also unique. Yet I believe you can find areas to use your God-given gifts to minister to the lives of others.

And now, if you'll excuse me, my kids and I have some cookies to bake.

---

https://bear.org/bear-facts/senses-and-abilities/
https://www.hhs.gov/sites/default/files/surgeon-general-social-connection-advisory.pdf

Rediscovering
DREAMS

Delight yourself in the Lord;

And He will give you the desires of your heart.

— Psalm 37:4 (NASB1995)

To accomplish great things
we must not only act, but also dream;
Not only plan, but also believe.

— Anatole France

CHAPTER THREE

My love affair with horses began when I was five years old. Several people used to ride their horses past our home. There were three horses in the bunch, including a beautiful bay, a coppery chestnut, and a dappled gray. The horses towered over me. At the time I was small enough to walk under their stomachs. Their thoughtful owners gave Laurel and me rides. Even though they frightened me, the animals captured my attention and my heart. Through the years, my desire to own a horse grew until it was an obsession.

Laurel loved horses as much as I did. We talked about horses. We read books about horses. We watched movies about horses. We dreamt about horses. Thankfully, Mom and Dad didn't ever discourage our dreams of owning a horse. In fact, as an optimist and dreamer himself, Dad encouraged us to dream big. He often quoted the Scripture found in Psalm 37:3 which says, "Delight yourself in the Lord, and He will give you the desires of your heart." I never doubted I would have a horse. I knew it was just a matter of time. My dream would become a reality.

Mom also encouraged our pursuit. Yet she was more of a realist than Dad. "You can have a horse someday," Mom agreed, "yet you will need to figure out a way to pay for it. Horses are expensive!" And they are! Horses eat a lot! On top of food expenses are boarding, vet exams, and farrier visits. This reality didn't deter us. Laurel and I joyfully agreed and started planning. What could we do to earn the money to finance our dream?

Laurel came up with the idea of a pet-sitting business. We were ten years old. At that point, we had transitioned out of public school and back into homeschooling. We enjoyed many aspects of schooling at home, especially the added flexibility with our schedules. We presented our idea to Dad and Mom. Both were incredibly supportive. Mom's support surprised us. She didn't even like animals! Even our family dog and pet rabbits stayed outdoors. I later asked Mom why she consented. "You were so focused on your goal that I didn't have the heart to say no," she commented. Isn't it fascinating that our belief swayed her decision?

After they approved, we moved forward quickly. We ran an ad in our local newspaper, *The Katahdin Times*. Soon we received our first pets, Max and Schnitzel. The elderly dogs were mild-mannered and gentle. We thoroughly enjoyed caring for them. They remained our most consistent customers for many years. In addition to dogs, we cared for cats, birds, and horses. We tenaciously saved our hard-earned money, and our bank account started to grow.

Our confidence blossomed. With each passing year, we had more faith that our dream would come true. The waiting was challenging at times, but we didn't doubt that we'd get a horse. Our pet-caring business prepared us for the responsibility of horse care. Whenever we received customers, Mom entrusted the pets' care to us. We fed and watered them daily. We walked and cared for them. We scheduled new clients. All of these tasks cultivated responsibility.

In addition, we learned as much as we could about horses. We read books about horsemanship. We took riding lessons for several semesters. We weren't aware of anyone in Millinocket who gave lessons, so we traveled to Sherman. Mom had a connection there. Sherman, Maine is over 30 miles north of Millinocket. The drive to the farm took about 45 minutes. I feel so grateful for Mom's commitment to her family. Her sacrifice allowed us to develop riding skills. All in all, Laurel and I stayed open to opportunities as they presented themselves. One of the most incredible connections was a man named Mr. Hartwell.

Mom met Mr. Hartwell at Millinocket Regional Hospital. Mom worked as a float nurse, and he worked in radiology. Within several years of employment, she interacted with all of Millinocket's health care staff. She knew everyone casually. When Mom discovered that Mr. Hartwell owned several horses, she immediately thought of Laurel and me. She asked if he would allow us to help him with his horses. Mr. Hartwell agreed.

One of my mentors says, "When the student is ready, the teacher appears." Mr. Hartwell was that teacher for us. When we met him, Mr. Hartwell immediately felt like a grandfather. He was about twenty years older than Mom and Dad, and he valued children. He and his wife were raising their grandson, who was several years younger than me. They lived only two blocks away from our house. Mr. Hartwell was a man of few words, but he clearly identified with our love for horses. He took Laurel and me under his wing and quietly mentored us in horsemanship.

One of Mr. Hartwell's daughters really liked horses. Throughout her childhood, Mr. Hartwell bred and showed Arabians. His daughter had since married and left town, but he still owned several beautiful Arabians. Mr. Hartwell boarded the horses just outside of town at a location known as "The Hovel." Located on Staceyville Road, the horse property occupied the northernmost boundary of town. And it was only two miles from our house.

The Hovel contained a modest collection of barns and paddocks. Horse owners leased and maintained their properties independently of one another. Hovel boarders agreed to adhere to bylaws and regulations. The Hovel association functioned similarly to the HOAs of today.

At that time, Staceyville Road was an active logging road. So, logging trucks occasionally rattled by. The secluded area maintained an atmosphere of activity. Because of this, the barns sat about a quarter of a mile away from the dangerous, dirt road.

Mr. Hartwell leased several Hovel lots. He boarded three of his horses in the Hovel's largest barn. His fence line encompassed multiple lots. His property was beautiful and meticulously maintained. We weekly accompanied Mr. Hartwell to his barn for the horses' afternoon feedings. Sometimes he picked us up after work. Most times, we walked the two blocks to his house and waited until he was ready.

We assisted Mr. Hartwell in several ways. We fed and watered the horses. We groomed them too. After we gained experience, Mr. Hartwell even let us ride his two mares, Stephanie and Veraina. Discovering riding options in Millinocket was a dream come true!

Stephanie was Mr. Hartwell's oldest Arabian. She was a creamy white color and small — nearly the size of a pony. While ponies are oftentimes frisky, Stephanie's personality was kind and gentle. She enjoyed a leisurely pace in her later years. Stephanie liked to lie down in the sunshine so her white coat often picked up dust and dirt. Even so, she was beautiful.

We also rode Veraina. Veraina was much younger than Stephanie. Her coat was white as well, though it contained undertones of gray dapples. Veraina hadn't had much training and did not share Stephanie's sweet demeanor. Her energy demanded our full attention. Laurel and I always welcomed a challenge, so we still enjoyed Veraina. All in all, Mr. Hartwell's generosity allowed Laurel and me to experience a little piece of Heaven on earth.

In addition to our weekly Hovel work, Mr. Hartwell periodically took us to horse auctions. The auction site was over an hour away from Millinocket. The three of us drove to the auctions in his Ford pickup. His green truck was old.

It had a manual transmission and one slippery leather bench seat. The interior maintained a musty smell of fresh earth and horses. We rode most of the way without talking. Mr. Hartwell played country music quietly over the radio.

Once we arrived, Mr. Hartwell sat in the stands. Laurel and I wandered around the paddocks. We walked slowly through the aisles of horses. We admired the beautiful animals. We dreamed of owning a horse one day. During one of these auctions, Mr. Hartwell bought us a saddle and bridle. His unprecedented generosity blessed us beyond measure.

Although he rarely said a word, Mr. Hartwell's gentle manner trained us in ways words couldn't. We watched him and learned so much. He influenced us greatly in everything related to horses. Mr. Hartwell constantly reminded us of the hard work that accompanies horse ownership. He allowed us to experience the joys and the difficulties of caring for horses. For example, the Hovel didn't have running water. A hand pump supplied this commodity. During the summer months, we easily accessed the water. However, along with the subzero temperatures of winter, the pump froze. During these months, Hovel boarders hauled water from home. We helped Mr. Hartwell with this task.

After several years under Mr. Hartwell's tutelage, we received a phone call from one of Dad's hunting clients. A robust Italian from New York City, "Fat Tony" was his nickname. Fat Tony raced Thoroughbreds. Thoroughbreds are a hotblooded breed known for their agility and speed. Many Thoroughbreds are quite young when they start training. Some begin racing as early as two years old. Due to the strenuous training, it's common for racehorses to develop injuries. Horses are expensive to maintain but even more expensive to rehab. Owners have to weigh the cost with the reward when their horses develop injuries. Many injured racehorses are discarded. A fortunate Thoroughbred is adopted. Those less fortunate are euthanized.

Due to his connections, Fat Tony remained knowledgeable about local racehorses. When he could, he helped re-home injured horses. He knew Laurel and I wanted a horse. So Fat Tony considered horses that might be a good fit. There were several instances when he offered horses. Yet finances and timing weren't quite right and we had to turn him down. But in the spring of 1996, everything came together.

I answered the phone that day. "Hello?" I replied. "Are you ready for a horse?" Fat Tony's exuberant voice bellowed through the phone line. Excitement rushed through my body. Laurel and I had finally saved enough money to consider a horse, so I knew this call could turn out differently than the others. "Yes!" I responded. Fat Tony then informed me of the situation.

"It's a colt," he explained. "The horse is only two years old, but he has a severe injury called bowed tendons." Even though he couldn't see my face, I nodded in understanding. Fat Tony went on to explain more about the horse's condition. Occurring in horses who experience chronic stress, this muscle injury requires adequate time to heal for optimal functionality in the future. The colt's owners decided to re-home him instead of nursing his recovery. Fat Tony knew the owner and immediately thought of us.

Laurel and I were ecstatic! Our dream was coming true! We were only 13 years old, so we were naive and immature in many ways. We didn't quite comprehend the responsibility of our agreement. However, so many wonderful people collaborated with us as we figured out last-minute details.

Everything transpired quickly. My grandfather, Pop-pop Reed, was a truck driver. He also loved horses. He agreed to drive the colt from New York to Maine. Pop-pop borrowed a horse trailer and picked up the horse from the city. Then he transported and cared for the animal during the tedious drive north. Laurel and I didn't yet have a barn or property for our rescued animal! However, we knew the details would work themselves out. Miraculously, they did.

Can you guess who helped us with a barn? That's right! Mr. Hartwell. Once he heard of our situation, Mr. Hartwell generously offered one of his vacant barns. The barn was simple. It had one stall and a tiny tack room. The paddock was quaint, too. But it was all perfect for our new horse. Mr. Hartwell required no rent while we used the property. His expectation was simple: take care of every-thing as if it was our own. We did.

We thoroughly cleaned the barn from top to bottom. We neatly arranged a grain bin, saddle, bridle, and grooming tools in the tack room. We stacked dozens of hay bales into the loft. We purchased our own wheelbarrow and rakes. We cleared away debris from the paddock and removed anything that could cause harm.

Looking back on that time, I am amazed at God's goodness. He provided solutions for our dreams — more than we could have ever asked or imagined. With tears in his eyes, Dad quietly reminded us of the promise he'd spoken over us since we were young. "You've delighted yourselves in the Lord, Lizzy and Laurel, and God has given you the desires of your heart."

Our two-year-old racehorse arrived within weeks of Fat Tony's phone call. We joyfully welcomed him to his new home. Racehorses have prolific names. Our horse's original name was "A Special Paddock." We didn't mind his name but it was quite a mouthful, so Laurel and I changed his name to Kedar, which in Hebrew means "dark."

Kedar was magnificent! His bay-colored coat shone like copper in the sun. His black mane and tail glistened like onyx. He had a small white star on his forehead and two alternating white socks on his legs. His body was powerful yet sleek — perfect for racing. He stood just over 16 hands high. When tacked up in his saddle, Laurel and I were unable to see over his back. True to his breed, Kedar was spirited! Young and untrained, he knew only one speed — fast! He had much to learn in the area of manners.

Despite his spunk, Laurel and I cherished our new horse. However, we almost lost him shortly after he arrived. That's when we discovered that fulfilled dreams don't guarantee smooth sailing.

As I mentioned, Kedar was recovering from bowed tendons. Laurel and I faithfully tended to him during his healing. We were so excited to ride him! Yet we patiently waited as he recovered. Spring turned to summer, and Kedar steadily improved.

One warm morning, we decided to give him a bath. The hand pump sat across from our barn. Yet collecting water was still quite tedious. So instead of hauling water, we just brought Kedar closer to the pump. While barns formed neat rows behind the pump, there were limited options for tethering. A metal gate spanned the width between two barns. It was conveniently located several strides behind the pump. It seemed quite secure, so we tied Kedar to it. After tying him up, we realized we'd forgotten several items in our barn. We momentarily left him unattended. That brief error in judgment led to disaster.

While we were at our barn, Kedar restlessly stepped on his trailing lead rope. He tangled his foot and began to panic. Rearing in fright, he dislodged the metal gate from between the barns. Frantic, he took off, tearing down Staceyville Road. The metal gate remained attached to Kedar's lead rope. With each stride, the gate thrashed his back legs.

Remember, this occurred before the invention of cell phones. We couldn't just make a call for help. Laurel and I had to use our limited judgment to save our horse.

Laurel grabbed a bucket of grain, hoping to stop him with food. She raced through the woods toward the adjacent Hovel. But Kedar didn't detour. He just continued racing down the uneven logging road.

I jumped on my 10-speed bike and pedaled as fast as I could, trying to keep up with the manic animal. Although I pedaled furiously, Kedar was much too fast for me. He quickly put space between us. Several miles into my pursuit, Kedar veered off the road and into the forest. I still don't know how he managed to run through the dense underbrush with the gate dragging behind him. I breathlessly pedaled on, recognizing this was my chance to catch up. But as he ran, Kedar instinctively turned himself around. He exited the forest behind me and barreled back toward the barn. I quickly changed directions, hoping he'd stay on the road until he reached my sister.

Back at the Hovel, Laurel heard Kedar's labored breathing and the grating gate coming closer and closer. When he came into view, Laurel shuddered at what she saw. Frothing, white sweat covered Kedar's entire body. Blood spewed from his back legs with each step. Once he reached her, Kedar stopped. He was too exhausted to run another step. His lungs labored upon each wheezing breath. Sobbing uncontrollably, Laurel separated Kedar from the gate. I reached her shortly after, and we walked him back to the barn together.

Near the end of this disastrous adventure, Mr. Hartwell arrived for the afternoon feeding. He helped us save Kedar. The details surrounding Kedar's rescue are still a bit foggy. Somehow the vet arrived. He solemnly informed us about the seriousness of the situation. Kedar nearly ran himself to death. He'd lost a significant amount of blood from the punctured arteries. His body succumbed to shock, and his recovery looked bleak.

For several hours, Kedar struggled for each breath. We gently bathed his overheated body, trying to cool him down. Later that day, his breathing finally normalized. However, he remained lying down and wouldn't move. Over the next several weeks, Laurel and I diligently nursed him back to health. We administered antibiotics, changed his bandages, and monitored his progress. Miraculously, Kedar recovered.

I feel so thankful that God intervened despite our err in judgment. The accident was our fault. We knew never to leave horses unattended. If we followed that wisdom, Kedar's accident could have been prevented. This instance reminds me of God's grace and mercy. So many times, He fills in your gaps even when you're at fault.

After his injuries healed, Kedar's strength and spirit returned. Then we started to ride. Though he was saddle broke, Kedar didn't have much formal training. Remember, he used to be a racehorse! He only knew one speed! My first time in the saddle wasn't anything like what I imagined it would be.

The Hovel's riding arena was positioned several hundred meters away from the barns. It paralleled Staceyville Road. Beautifully surrounded by forest, the arena provided a level area for riders to exercise their horses. Riders walked away from the Hovel down a small hill to access the fenced ring. It was strategically built away from the distraction of the other horses. However, horses are herd animals. They frequently form attachments. When away from the herd, they often feel separation anxiety. Their behavior may become erratic when removed from their familiar environment.

Kedar lived independently, and yet he formed attachments with his Hovel mates. He expressed abundant anxiety during his first several outings. Combining this with his interest in speed, Kedar challenged our riding abilities. Our first time in the arena, Dad watched. He monitored Kedar and me. Saddled and ready to go, Kedar nervously glanced back and forth. He looked manic. He pranced around, hardly standing still long enough for me to mount.

Once on his back, I struggled to maintain control. I felt his incredible power with each stride. I started him at a brisk walk, and I held the reins tightly to control his pace. He finally relaxed, so I decided to trot. I gently encouraged him with my heels. All he needed was that light pressure, and he took off like a flash of lightning! He galloped around the arena at full throttle! I struggled to regain control, but Kedar had other ideas. After several laps, he abruptly stopped at the arena gate. The change in momentum threw me over the fence. Excited for his freedom, Kedar took off once more! He bucked! He kicked! He ran circles until his energy expired.

Shaken from the fall, I felt incredibly frightened. Thankfully, I was not hurt. Yet I realized how spirited Kedar actually was. The experience reminded me that I had so much to learn. And Kedar needed extensive training.

After Kedar stopped, I caught him and mounted once more. My body still trembled with fear. Yet I knew that I must exercise authority over the situation. The "wildly take off, stop abruptly, and toss rider over the gate" remained Kedar's favorite trick to dismount any unwelcome riders. Ultimately, we did learn to manage and direct his youthful energy into productive activities. Later on, we introduced him to the sport of jumping. He loved it! Kedar became an accomplished jumper and competed in many shows after he transitioned to other families.

Our time with Kedar was memorable and special in so many ways. First of all, I realized that dreams are worth imagining — and worth pursuing. As a young girl, my parents encouraged my lofty ideas. Dad always modeled this trait. He wasn't afraid to think outside the box and then put action behind his ideas. To this day, Dad continues to inspire me. Recently, he pursued his lifelong dream of owning and operating a bakery. He often talked about this dream while I was young. I watched him open his first bakery while in his '50s. Then he launched his second bakery in his '60s. Dad is one of my examples of a dreamer. He allows himself to use his imagination and designs his life accordingly. Dad's age and other hindrances don't stop him.

Mom enjoys living life within the lines. Yet she is her family's biggest fan. She always encourages and wholeheartedly supports whatever pursuits her family thinks up. Dad and Mom both continually encourage me to dream. When I shared my idea of writing this book, Dad's approval motivated me to begin. As I developed each chapter, Dad and Mom excitedly read the pages. Their enthusiasm encouraged me to keep going.

Their influence teaches me that if you're a dreamer, it's vitally important to surround yourself with people who believe in you. I've heard it said that a person's association determines their destiny. I've had to ask myself many times, *Are my closest friends encouraging me to run after my God-given dreams? Or are they discouraging me and deterring my passions?* Our dreams can be helped or hindered by those around us. I've experienced both.

A mentor of mine says, "You are only one or two powerful relationships away from dramatically altering your life forever." Have you experienced this truth? I certainly have. I just think of Kedar's story! I think of my parents who supported my sister's and my efforts when we started our pet caring business. I think of "Fat Tony" who remembered Laurel and me when he discovered Kedar. I think of Pop-pop who transported Kedar from New York to Maine. And I think of Mr. Hartwell, who so gently took us under his wing, taught us everything he knew about horsemanship, and generously gave us his extra barn. All these people equipped and empowered us to accomplish more than we could have ever asked or imagined.

Thanks to Kedar, I learned early that persistence doesn't end once a dream manifests. That's when grit and resilience truly begin. We worked relentlessly to provide for Kedar's needs. Not only did we have our pet-caring business and other jobs throughout high school, but Kedar required daily care. From the time he was placed in our hands until we left for college five years later, Laurel and I made the four-mile round trip twice a day to the Hovel. We fed and watered him in the morning and at night. We received rides from Mr. Hartwell and our parents, but we made many of the trips on our own. Like many dreams, taking care of Kedar was incredibly challenging and all-consuming. But, for the most part, it was also a total joy.

Can you think of a dream that required continued grit after you launched the endeavor? This book is an example. From the time I was twelve years old, I wanted to write a book. I thought life would slow down, giving me time to write. I thought an opportunity would present itself. What was I thinking? Each season got busier and busier. Instead of time slowing down, it sped up. Years slipped away, and writing didn't happen.

Have you ever heard the phrase, "Don't confuse the decision-making process with the problem-solving process?" My mentor repeats this frequently. "Decide *what to do*," he says, "and then figure out *how to do it*." I applied this principle when I wrote this book.

When I started writing, the timing wasn't great. I was navigating work-related challenges. I was experiencing mental unrest and emotional upheaval. I suffered from insomnia. Even as I edit these sentences a year later, I am wading through other health challenges. Yet perspective is everything, isn't it? I decided to start writing, and the timing worked itself out. Remember I struggled with insomnia? Well, that worked in my favor as I often wrote before the sun came up. The present health problems demand rest. So instead of running in the morning, as is my normal habit, I'm editing my book. Despite the many challenges, this project has been a total joy. It renewed my values. It refreshed my spirit. It reminded me to dream again.

As I've worked to achieve my dreams, I've recognized the importance of my thoughts and words. As I mentioned earlier, Laurel's and my life revolved around horses. We read about horses. Talked about horses. Wrote stories about horses. Watched horse movies and drew horse pictures. Horses were everything we thought and spoke about.

Today, many authors and speakers teach about the power of the subconscious mind and the spoken word.

Unbeknownst to us, we implemented these principles. We used them in our favor. Our mind painted pictures of a subsequent reality. Our words planted seeds for our future. And those seeds eventually brought a harvest. It was not by accident that we eventually received Kedar. I believe a spiritual principle brought it to pass. Hebrews 11:1, 3 says, "Now faith is confidence in what we hope for and assurance of what we cannot see...By faith we understand that the universe was formed at God's command, so that what is seen was not made out of what was visible." Initially we didn't know how all the details would work out. Yet we had faith that they would. We moved forward one day at a time. We looked toward the future with expectation. We worked with assurance. We spoke about our dream to others. We had a childlike faith that confidently believed.

In my forties, faith doesn't come as naturally to me as it once did. I sometimes struggle to believe. At times I lose hope. *Is it better to bury my dreams than live with the disappointment of unfulfilled desires?* This question plagued me this past year. I tried burying my hopes. Ignoring my dreams. Pretending they didn't matter anymore. Even though they did. And that's where I was when I started this book.

Proverbs 13:12 says, "Hope deferred makes the heart sick, but a longing fulfilled is a tree of life." I must admit, I lost hope in many areas of my life. My heart was sick. And my sick heart eventually affected my body. Yet, as I write these stories — my story — dreams are resurfacing. Faith is returning. Hope is healing my heart and my body. And God reminded me I don't have to have a mountain of faith — a mustard seed size will do. Can you relate to any of this?

Can I encourage you to keep believing?! Keep hoping?! Keep dreaming?!

My favorite book on this topic is *The Dream Giver.* Author Bruce Wilkinson shares a short yet powerful parable. It centers around an individual named Ordinary. Ordinary leaves the land of Familiar in search of his Big Dream. Excited for his journey, he doesn't realize the obstacles that lie ahead. Along his journey, he encounters Bullies. He enters a Wasteland. Fights Giants. Experiences rejection. Suffers injuries. And he nearly loses hope. Yet, Ordinary never gives up. He eventually enters The Land of Promise. Here Ordinary realizes that he is no longer Ordinary. He is Somebody. Yet he discovers it wasn't his journey that changed him into Somebody. He was Somebody all along. He was born to accomplish Great Things.

You and I were born to accomplish Great Things too.

This story reminded me that I am not ordinary. Neither are you. You are Somebody. You were born to accomplish Great Things. I believe God planted dreams inside your heart. Are some of your dreams personal desires? That's okay! Are your dreams so big they frighten you? That's okay too! Whatever dream lies within your heart — whether minuscule or magnificent — I believe it's valid. Can you give yourself permission to dream again? Can you envision your life outside the lines?

I encourage you to surround yourself with people who undergird you. Guard yourself from those who tear you down. Persevere through hardships. Equip yourself with tenacity. Use the power of your subconscious mind. Plant words of faith into your future. And keep God at the center of it all. Because He's the One who placed those dreams in your heart. I experienced the fulfillment of my horse dream when Fat Tony gave Laurel and me Kedar. I am currently watching my book dream blossom and bear fruit. I believe the same for you too. You will eventually reap a harvest — if you do not give up.

Rediscovering
COMPASSION

Rejoice with those who rejoice, and weep with those who weep. Be sensitive to each other's needs — don't think yourselves better than others, but make humble people your friends.

Don't be conceited...and to the extent that it depends on you, live at peace with all people.

— Romans 12:15, 16, 18 (CJB)

Your true character
is most accurately measured
by how you treat those
who can do 'Nothing' for you.

— Mother Teresa

Wᴇ had a revolving door in our home. Friends and neighbors walked in and out with ease. Throughout the ten years we lived on Knox Street, my parents didn't even have a house key. Unless we were away on a trip, we left the front door unlocked. We never locked the backdoor. Not only did Mom and Dad leave the house doors open, but they left their hearts open as well. I witnessed a compassion in my parents that extended from our home and into the lives of others. Dad had many intentional conversations with us about genuine humility. "We're not better than anyone else," he would say. Romans 12:15–18 is a Scripture that we read often around our breakfast table. My parents' lives embodied it.

Dad is spontaneous. He is also very generous and hospitable. Mom learned to accommodate these traits. She remained ready to host unexpected guests for mealtime.

Most often visitors joined us for supper. Other times, we hosted them for breakfast or lunch.

Dad's businesses provided him with many opportunities to meet people. Sometimes they had challenging backgrounds. When needed, Dad willingly set aside his work, poured several cups of coffee, and lent a listening ear. At times he left projects forgotten. Yet he didn't leave people that way. Dad provided friendship and compassion to whomever crossed his path. Pretense wasn't a temptation for him.

I have so many memories of special friends. My Knox Street friendships were really unique. For starters there was Tim*. Remember the days of newspapers and paper routes? Well, that was Tim's job. He serviced our neighborhood. Tim was interesting. He was more than a little awkward, yet he persisted in his pursuit of sales. Tim maintained our neighborhood route for a year or so. Throughout that time, Dad and Mom didn't purchase any newspapers from Tim. However, they pursued a relationship with him.

Tim became one of our breakfast guests. Mom always cooked something warm and delicious in the morning, and Dad routinely invited Tim in for eggs, pancakes, or oatmeal. Tim sat, talked, and laughed. He often stayed throughout our morning devotions. At that time, I didn't quite understand why he joined us. I even felt slightly irritated that we had someone who was nearly a stranger sitting with us at breakfast.

I used to wonder, *Why do we have to entertain this awkward young man? Why is he even here? Doesn't he have his own family to eat breakfast with?* Now I admire Dad's kindness. I think Tim just desired a listening ear. Dad accepted Tim and gave him a safe place to belong. While our family lost touch with Tim, I hope the time around our table positively impacted him for years to come. It certainly left an imprint on my young heart. I started to realize that life consists of caring for others, even when they may be very different from you.

The next special friendship started one frosty, winter day when I was only 10 years old. On this particular day, I wandered up and down Knox Street, playing in the snowbanks on my own. In the midst of my adventure, I paused in front of a neighbor's home. A giant snowbank loomed in their front yard, and I wanted to continue my game. However, unfavorable rumors about this family circulated around the neighborhood. I knew I should steer clear of their property. Even so, I maneuvered my way up the prolific mound of snow. At the top I discovered a young girl. She was not more than four years old and sat alone in her fluffy pink snowsuit. Blue-green eyes peered at me in surprise, and blonde hair curled wispily from under her hat. Round cheeks glowed pink with cold.

I introduced myself and discovered the girl's name was Haven*. Haven was friendly and sweet. She wasn't aloof or rough as the rumors eluded. I excitedly returned home and announced who I'd met. Helene and Amber immediately dressed in their snow gear and ran over to the snowbank. They introduced themselves to Haven and played with her the rest of the afternoon. From then on, they developed a special friendship with her. In fact, we all joyfully embraced Haven as family. For the next ten years, she became the most frequent visitor to our home. Haven played with my sisters for hours each day and rarely wanted to go home.

We later discovered that Haven's home life was a bit challenging. However, when things became unpleasant, she crossed the street and invited herself in. Our family wasn't perfect, yet I think Haven felt cherished and loved when she walked through our front door. We Reed girls pretended she was our fifth sister. Even after we moved away from Maine, we welcomed Haven. She's visited several times. Like Tim, our paths haven't crossed for many years. However, we treasure our memories with Haven.

Multiple other neighborhood girls experienced the same welcoming. Our kitchen table often hosted not only my four siblings and me, but two or three other kids. Ironically, Mom preferred a quiet home atmosphere. She would have loved to prioritize her own family's needs over the needs of the neighborhood, but she extended grace and welcomed the Knox Street kids as her own. She was an incredible example of caring over convenience.

When we started high school, Laurel and I felt the tension of transition. Ready for a change, we finished home-schooling at the end of ninth grade. We started attending Stearns High School as sophomores. Though we considered ourselves a part of the community, we were not natives of Millinocket. Most Millinocket kids have been together since preschool. By the time high school starts, their friendships are already well-established.

Laurel and I made some friends at Katahdin Elementary School in fourth grade, yet we still felt like outsiders and wondered where we belonged. Laurel and I were well-liked and got along with everyone. Despite this, we had few close friends. Some of our relational awkwardness stemmed from personal convictions. We didn't follow the crowd, and at times peers misunderstood our values. However, once at Stearns, we developed special friendships with several classmates. Maria and Amy became dear friends. Another cherished friendship was with a remarkable young woman named Chiemi.

A foreign exchange student from Japan, Chiemi arrived in Millinocket in 1997. I originally met her at the home of her host family as I babysat their two biological daughters. Because I've always been fascinated by other cultures, Chiemi immediately intrigued me. Initially, Chiemi spoke minimal English. Even so, we instantly liked each other. I quickly introduced her to Laurel, and our special friendship blossomed.

Chiemi was beautiful inside and out. She had a warm personality, a magnetic smile, and sparkling eyes. At first, the language barrier caused Chiemi to act quiet and reserved. Yet, once her English improved, Chiemi overflowed with animated personality. And humor — lots of humor! I can still remember her musical laugh. We often giggled incessantly whenever we spent time together. Everyone who knew Chiemi absolutely adored her.

Laurel, Chiemi, and I became the best of friends that year. Several reasons contributed to our special friendship. The three of us transitioned to Stearns High School in the same year. As mentioned before, newcomers at Stearns are rare, so this promptly drew us together. Additionally, though we were in different grades, we shared several electives. Our time together at school was so much fun! Even more exciting was when we became neighbors. This aspect impacted our friendship the most. Shortly after school started, Chiemi transferred from her initial host family to our neighbor's home only three doors away. Anne and Randy Jackson hosted her for the remainder of the year. Because of this, we saw each other even more frequently.

We enjoyed so many fun experiences that year! The highlights revolved around our shared love of music. Chiemi taught us how to speak, sing, and write Japanese. We spent hours rehearsing together. Everyone admired Chiemi's beautiful voice and charming spirit. When our trio performed a heartwarming Japanese song in our high school's annual talent show, we won first place! The entire year produced a magical scrapbook of memories.

Chiemi's inevitable departure loomed in the future. Despite this, we loved each other deeply and continually invested in our friendship. At the end of the school year, Chiemi returned to Japan. Laurel and I experienced heartbreaking sadness. Despite the heartache, I don't regret our friendship. To this day, that year remains one of the best years of my life.

My Chiemi memories remind me of the unparalleled joys of friendship. Chiemi has visited the States twice over the past two decades. Both times, Laurel and I reconnected with her. Although our busy lives now make communication a bit sporadic, we still delight in any interaction we have with each other.

Am I still forming friendships with people who may be in a transient season? Am I still pursuing people despite the risk of loss? I considered these questions as I wrote about my memories of Chiemi.

Around the same time I met Chiemi, I developed another unique friendship. I met David* when I was a young eighth grader. While we'd lived on the same street for five years, our paths hadn't crossed. David was almost six years my senior, so he was in a very different stage of life. Not only was he in a different season of life, but David was quite different from me in every way. Popular, athletic, and entertaining, David lived life in the fast lane. He seemed to have everything any young man could want.

David's family was one of our pet-sitting clients, so we initially met because of their dog. She was a beautiful Husky and had lots of energy! I watched David rollerblade around the neighborhood as he exercised her. It looked like so much fun, and I wanted to do this too! So I asked David's mom if he might consider teaching me. She asked David for me, and he agreed. From there, I was introduced to the risky activity — and to my neighbor's son. The sport proved a little too adventurous for me. I experienced a painful — and very embarrassing — crash my first time out! I decided to set it aside. Initially, because David was so much older than me, I also set aside any notions of friendship. It wasn't until months later that our friendship developed.

The summer before my sophomore year, I had an upsetting conversation with Mom. One day she returned from visiting with David's mom, and she was distraught. When I asked what was wrong, Mom said, "David's having some mental health challenges. He attempted to end his life..." Her voice broke as she relayed the information.

Mom's words left my mind reeling. I felt shocked. How could this confident young man, who appeared to have life figured out, feel so troubled and hopeless? So hopeless that he no longer wanted to live? My heart and spirit exploded with compassion. My first thought was, *He needs Jesus.* The next thought soon followed: *He needs a friend.* So, with a limited and immature view of mental illness, I naively believed that a friendship with David could eradicate some of the negative effects of his diagnosis.

While my perception proved inaccurate, David's and my friendship was one of the joys of my teen years. It was a journey of unforgettable fun. We played music together. We participated in youth group activities. And we experienced fishing adventures with Dad. Despite his challenges, David embodied enthusiasm for life. I admired his ambitions and dreams for the future. Our group of friends enjoyed many evenings playing music at his home. It was our favorite thing to do together.

David's parents supported his passion and gift for music, so they converted the upstairs of their garage into a music studio. David's friends played music there. Instruments of every kind were organized into an artistic array. When people walked into David's studio, it seemed as if the instruments beckoned musicians to play. On many evenings, rhythms of drumbeats echoed throughout the neighborhood. When I wasn't personally involved in the musical collaborations, the melodic beats lulled me to sleep. To this day, I love listening to drums.

I was much more reserved than my friend. Yet through our "jamming sessions," David taught my sister and me to be creative. He encouraged us to explore beyond classical music. To play chords instead of sheet music. To improvise when playing blues. Oh, how I disliked soloing during the blues! I learned so much about music from David. To this day, I implement what he taught me when figuring out piano pieces.

It was because of our friendship that David accepted my invitations to church. Unbeknownst to me, his dear mother prayed for David for many years. In the fall of 1997, David decided to pursue a personal relationship with Jesus. From that point on, he joined us for church and youth group outings. He even played music with Laurel and me at church. David's faith carried him through many difficult seasons.

From our dynamic relationship, I discovered that friendships can sometimes produce insurmountable pain. David experienced significant challenges because of mental illness. He struggled to maintain stability and vacillated in and out of psychiatric hospitals. I experienced deep internal pain watching this. David's problems weren't easily solved, and my young heart wrestled with questions that didn't have easy answers.

Why do some people have more problems than others? I asked myself. *Will David have to deal with mental illness for the rest of his life? Will he ever find rest outside of his disease?* And the question that initiated the most unrest I asked because of my faith: *God, you've healed so many in the past and present. Why haven't you healed my friend?* My friendship with David taught me to be aware of everyone around me

— not just those on the fringes. Sometimes it's the people who appear to have it all that have the deepest needs.

The Latin root word for compassion comes from "compati," which means to "suffer with." And "suffer with" my friend, I did. In her book, *The Gifts of Imperfection*, Brene Brown writes extensively about compassion, connection, and courage. She says that the heart of compassion is acceptance. She concludes that the better we are at accepting not only others but ourselves, the more compassionate we become. I can say with honesty that I wasn't very good at accepting myself or others during my teen years. More often than not, I tried to fix the problems — and people — around me. As I matured, I began to cultivate compassion. I extended empathy. Learned how to accept reality. Since then, truth has intersected my painful questions. It started to transform my worldview.

Isn't caring deeply for humanity the very heartbeat of Jesus? And doesn't Christ foster friendship even when the relationship isn't fully reciprocated? He ministered with compassion. He empathized with humanity's brokenness. He experienced the pain of rejection. He loved despite the outcome. Jesus is the most beautiful example of loving without limits, caring despite the consequences, and pursuing relationships regardless of the reward.

Kent M. Kieth wrote a poem called *The Paradoxical Commandments*. It beautifully illustrates these truths. The following is the revised version:

People are often unreasonable, illogical, and self-centered;
Forgive them anyway.
If you are kind, people may accuse you of
selfish, ulterior motives;
Be kind anyway.
If you are successful, you will win some false friends
and some true enemies;
Succeed anyway.
If you are honest and frank, people may cheat you;
Be honest and frank anyway.
What you spend a year building,
someone could destroy overnight.
Build anyway.
If you find serenity and happiness, they may be jealous;
Be happy anyway.
The good you do today, people will forget tomorrow;
Do good anyway.
Give the world the best you have,
and it may never be enough;
Give the world the best you have anyway.
You see, in the final analysis, it is between you and God,
It was never between you and them anyway.

Because of these friendships, I came to see that while people are unique, they are also very much the same. If we could peel back the emotional layers and peer into the souls of humanity, I think people would be indistinguishable. I believe every one of us hungers to belong, desires compassion, and craves love. Simply put, my friendships on Knox Street taught me to rejoice when others rejoice, weep when they weep, and make humble people my friends (Romans 12:15–18).

Of course, I am not advocating for dysfunctional or abusive relationships. There are times when we need boundaries. Being a compassionate person doesn't negate holding others accountable for their actions. Those unique situations aside, can I encourage you to live a life of compassion? Can you love unconditionally when it doesn't make sense? Can you permit yourself to care deeply despite the potential heartache? Will you value others unselfishly when nothing may be gained in return?

Thankfully, David continues to fight for his life. He maintains an amazing resolve to live each day, moment by beautiful moment. David's tenacity inspires me. He continues to live by faith, despite the darkness that at times clouds his creative mind. David periodically reaches out and thanks our family for the positive impact we had on his life. He recently reminded me, "Keep letting God's light shine, for you never know what darkness will be dispelled." David's words frequently replay in my mind. They remind me to keep focusing on others. To keep building friendships.

As an adult, I've carried on the Reed tradition of a revolving door. My family has frequent visitors during mealtimes. I invite neighbors in for tea. Neighborhood kids come and go with ease. At times my husband teases me, "Elizabeth, you no longer live in Millinocket! We're in a city now! Please lock the door!" I'll admit I'm still breaking my habit of leaving my house unlocked! However, I want to maintain the habit of leaving my heart unlocked.

I live in Colorado Springs now. It's very transient. The military bases and mountains draw thousands of new people each year. I have many opportunities to form new friendships, yet I don't always do this well. I sometimes get caught up in my never-ending to-do list. I sometimes find myself prioritizing projects over people. Sound familiar?

Then there are other times when I don't want to pursue people. Sometimes it's just too painful. Friends come — and then go. Other times I think people are my friends — until they aren't. Then there are friends I care for deeply. And these friends have problems. Problems I can't fix. Seeing their pain hurts so much. As I thought about this, I wondered, *How many of my anxious feelings this past year stemmed from relational challenges?*

As I mentally reviewed the year, I discovered that much of my internal angst revolved around relationships. I had many misunderstandings. Even betrayal. These situations caused feelings of anxiety and anger and pain. Then there were friends I loved deeply. Friends who needed help, yet there was little I could do. Friends similar to Haven and David. As I walked alongside them in the midst of their circumstances, my heart suffered with them. And I wasn't sure I could handle any more pain.

In the midst of my reflection, Jesus spoke to my heart. *"Elizabeth, I love people even more than you do. Let me carry them. Let me carry you. Cast your cares on me."*

What a beautiful reminder. God hasn't called us to shoulder people or their pain. And thankfully, He hasn't asked us to fix their problems either. I believe we are called to walk in humble acceptance of ourselves and of others. This is one of the beautiful serendipities of walking in a relationship with Jesus. He has compassion for you and everyone around you! You get to point humanity toward Him.

I must admit, I don't always understand friendships. Misunderstandings still happen. Sometimes I'm the cause of them! Yet my fond memories of Tim, Haven, Chiemi, and David inspire me to keep building friendships. Keep living compassionately. And keep shining God's light.

As you finish reading this chapter, can you think of someone who needs God's light? Can you extend love and grace in the midst of people's problems? Can you think of someone who "has it all" yet still needs a friend? Can you cultivate caring over convenience? Will you joyfully pursue people despite the risk of loss?

When I started writing the stories of my Knox Street friends, I didn't know what I'd find. Yet I discovered God working through my life. Ministering to others, some who were like me and others who were not, I discovered my life matters.

I've felt devoid of purpose for a long time. Wondering why I am even here. Why problems remain. Why friends come and go. My mentor says, "People come into your life for a reason, a season, or a lifetime." Reflecting on my neighborhood friendships, I can now see the value in each truth. Sometimes people cross your path for an instant. There's an exchange, and then you move on. Sometimes you walk with people for a longer stretch — a year or two. You make memories. Help each other through difficulties. Celebrate victories. And other times you have the privilege of journeying together for life. I am discovering the value of each type of friendship. There can be an impact in each interaction. And as I keep following Jesus, I pray He will work through me to impact many more.

As I close, the words from Isaiah 61 echo in my heart. The passage encourages readers to take their eyes off of themselves and put them on others, declaring hope, proclaiming freedom, and bestowing beauty to the hurting world. It's a prophetic announcement of Christ's work toward others while He walked on earth.

> "The Spirit of the Sovereign Lord is on me,
> Because the Lord has anointed me
> To proclaim good news to the poor...
> To bind up the brokenhearted,
> To proclaim freedom for the captives...
> To comfort all who mourn...
> To bestow on them a crown of beauty instead of ashes,
> The oil of gladness instead of mourning,
> And a garment of praise instead of a spirit of despair."
> Isaiah 61: 1–3 (NIV)

I've decided to adopt these verses as my mission and continue to extend compassion, friendship, and love to all who cross my path.

---

*Names changed for privacy.

Rediscovering
RESOURCEFULNESS

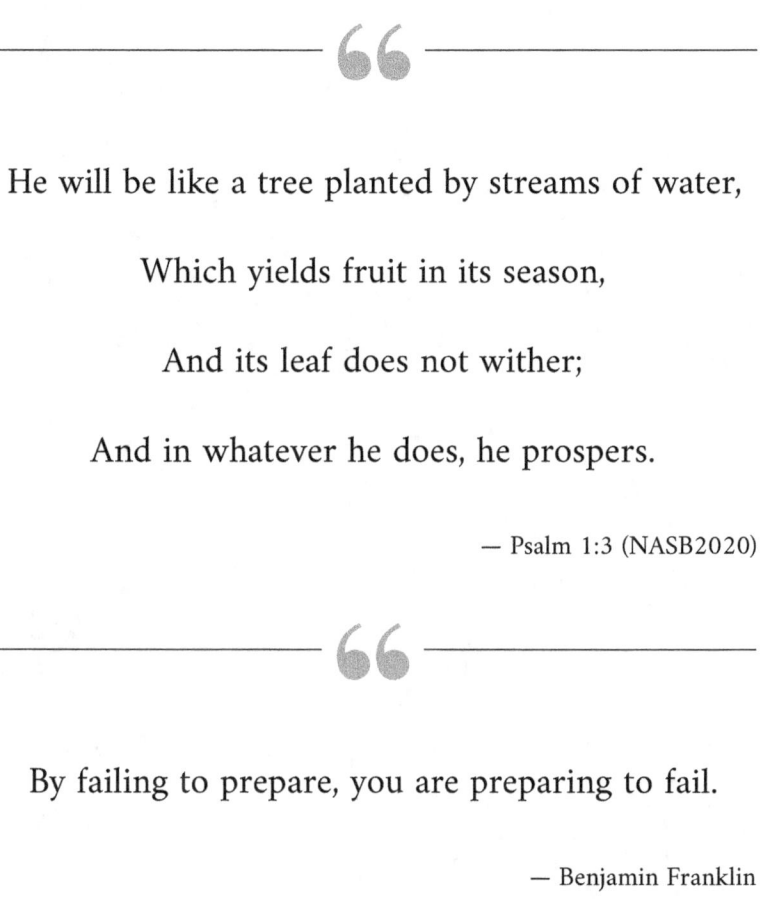

He will be like a tree planted by streams of water,

Which yields fruit in its season,

And its leaf does not wither;

And in whatever he does, he prospers.

— Psalm 1:3 (NASB2020)

By failing to prepare, you are preparing to fail.

— Benjamin Franklin

CHAPTER FIVE

As a young girl, I once asked my father if we were poor. My dad replied, "No, Lizzy. Poor is a state of mind. We are not poor." While I didn't quite comprehend the entirety of his answer, I understood the basis of what he communicated. That brief conversation settled my mind and heart to be at peace with our simple lifestyle.

Our house was small. I didn't have my own room. Neither did my sisters. Seth's bed sat in the hallway. We received hand-me-downs from friends. We didn't take extravagant vacations — or any vacations for that matter. We didn't have many material possessions. Yet my parents remained resourceful and optimistic in everything they did. I never felt poor.

My family worked together. We spent time together and took advantage of the natural bounty found within each season. It was through these rhythms of sowing, cultivating, and reaping that I discovered the beauty of God's abundant provision within nature.

To keep our lives simple, my parents planted a garden. That small backyard garden was our produce supplier. They worked diligently to cultivate it despite the short summer months. Readying and planting our garden were always family activities. When May arrived, the overnight temperatures finally climbed above freezing. Toward the end of that long-awaited month, Dad retrieved his rototiller from our storage shed and began the tedious task of turning over the earth. Mom assigned gardening roles. We worked alongside Mom and Dad, securing seeds in the moist soil. Whether or not we enjoyed the task, we knew better than to ask to avoid this duty.

I tended long rows of earth, handling little seeds of broccoli, carrots, beets, lettuce, and green beans. How I resented the green beans! The smooth seeds were easy enough to handle. It was knowing that the mature plants were always quite fruitful. Those small bean seeds meant a lot of work later in the summer!

Once the seeds were in the ground, we anxiously waited for them to take root. We watched with excitement as our backyard transformed into a life-giving biome. Throughout the summer, Mom assigned vegetable picking to Laurel and me. Remember the green beans? We were often required to fill a five-gallon bucket of beans before wandering off to play.

In August and September, the garden produced a never-ending cycle of work. Laurel and I picked vegetables every day. Mom worked relentlessly to preserve the fruits of our labor. She spent many evenings freezing vegetables. But we enjoyed our garden's bounty all winter long.

Our home had a simple room off the back of our kitchen. We called it the "Back Room." I think the previous homeowners built it as an afterthought. It was not well-insulated. The inefficient plywood floors were drafty during the freezing winter months, so Mom turned the space into a much-needed storage room.

Each wall in that room boasted a useful purpose. On one wall, long metal shelves held lots of extra food like pasta, canned goods, and our homemade preserves. On another wall, a small wooden shelf overflowed with homeschooling materials. A solitary toilet also sat there. The room was a very odd place for a toilet and using it during the winter months was nearly as chilly as an outhouse! The third wall housed two freezers packed to capacity with fresh fish, venison, our hand-picked vegetables, and fruit. The last wall had a single window. Next to the window stood the commercial mixer. We used this every week to make over-sized batches of chocolate chip cookies and bread.

To fill up the freezers in the back room, we picked lots of berries. Our family enjoyed the incredible, natural fruits that Maine had to offer. Wild raspberries, blackberries, and blueberries were bountiful in the woods surrounding Millinocket. Because of his guiding business, Dad spent considerable time scouting the forests around our town. He frequently returned with information about the best locations for picking wild fruit. As with gardening, our entire family participated in picking berries. Blueberries were our favorite. They often grew in previously logged or burned areas of forest. With the thick foliage cleared away, sunshine penetrated Maine's sandy soil. No matter where we went, the vegetation surrounding the blueberry patches was thick. I kept a close eye on Dad, Mom, and my siblings. I did not want to get separated as in Robert McCloskey's beloved book, *Blueberries for Sal.*

As with our gardening, my goal-oriented mom assigned fruit-picking quotas. We diligently worked to fill our buckets with berries. Mom joyfully reminded us of the reward that awaited our completed task — swimming! We frequently swam in Togue Pond. Located on the very outskirts of Baxter State Park, the crystal-clear water of Togue Pond remains freezing cold even during the summer months. It was so refreshing after the heat of berry-picking.

Once the blueberries were picked, it was time to clean and process them to be used later. Laurel and I often removed the debris that had mistakenly found its way into the family's berry buckets. This was not one of my favorite activities. Sometimes we completed this tedious task by hand. Other times, Laurel and I set up a system in our backyard. We slowly poured the berries from one bucket to another, using a fan to blow away leaves and sticks. That was a lot more interesting than picking out the debris by hand! After preparing the fruit, we filled up dozens of quart-sized Ziploc bags. Then we stacked these in the freezer alongside the vegetables. As the year went on, we turned those berries into homemade jam, pies, and crumbles. It was amazing to see our freezers packed to capacity with the fruits of our labor. Accomplishment and pride filled my young heart.

Not all of our produce came from our garden. Our family also participated in harvesting fresh, Maine potatoes. Potato harvests occur in Maine every autumn. Communities work together to gather abundant crops before the fall frost. Traditionally, potatoes were hand-picked. Machinery has since replaced that back-breaking labor. But even with machinery, hundreds of potatoes get left in the fields. Kindhearted to their core, many Maine farmers invite the surrounding communities to gather leftovers. A friend of Mom's invited our family to join. Always excited to harvest additional food, Mom eagerly accepted. We patiently traveled almost two hours to Maine's northernmost Aroostook County where potato farms are plentiful.

We arrived at the vast fields ready to work. We filled enough five-gallon buckets to sustain our family throughout the winter. I loved trudging through the fields, raking through the dirt, and discovering potatoes. It felt like a treasure hunt! We always returned home covered in dust, yet the task was so satisfying. These root vegetables were a staple in our home. We ate potatoes almost every day, either as hash browns for breakfast, diced in soups for lunch, or baked with pot roasts for supper.

Along with the fall came hunting season. Similar to enjoying homegrown produce and fruit, our family only ate fresh meat and fish. Store-bought poultry was rare in our house. We never purchased beef or fish. A talented outdoorsman, Dad harvested most of our meat. While we often fished together as a family, he usually hunted on his own. Mom continually edified Dad, praising his efforts to provide for our family. The meat sustained our growing family. Venison steaks, venison stew, and bear pot roast were favorite meals around our table. Brook trout were also a favorite. Mom and Dad thanked God daily for His constant provision. Their gratitude instilled a mindset that everything is a gift from God.

In addition to these food provisions, we also enjoyed wood from Maine's forests. My parents primarily heated our modest home with a wood stove, which was located in the cellar. Every fall, Dad ordered a load of wood. The dump truck dropped the wood into our driveway. Then Mom and Dad set aside several days to organize the wood. Dad split oversized logs. The rest of us tossed the overflowing mound from the driveway into the basement. For this to happen, Dad removed a tiny cellar window. Once the wood filled the basement, Dad taught us how to effectively stack the wood into sturdy rows. Our cellar became an obstacle course of lumber. All winter long, we enjoyed the warmth of the wood stove.

Mom made the most of the wood stove's heat when our clothes dryer broke. They didn't have the money for another one, so Mom dried the clothes in other ways. Throughout the sunny, summer months, Mom hung our clothes on the outdoor clothesline. While the task was quite inconvenient, I never heard Mom complain. She even commented about the wonderful fragrance of sun-dried clothes. The heat from the wood stove dried our clothes throughout the bitter-cold winter months. I admit that I didn't maintain the same attitude as Mom. I grumbled and complained about rigid jeans and stiff towels. *Everyone else has soft towels and pliable jeans,* I thought to myself. *Why can't my parents just get another dryer?* I now admire their commitment to stay out of debt. They did whatever was needed to make things work. I learned so much from their resourcefulness — though today I unashamedly enjoy soft jeans and plush towels!

Interestingly, other resourceful families surrounded my family. The Salvias were one of these families. My parents met Cliff and Donna when they lived in New York. They had three kids at the time. Their oldest daughter, Summer, was my closest childhood friend. The Salvias moved from New York to Maine several years after my parents.

The Salvias didn't settle in Millinocket but instead lived in the forests surrounding East Corinth. Similar to our family, they didn't have a house or jobs when they moved. Cliff, a creative carpenter and entrepreneur, decided they were going to design and build their own home. From scratch. This was not completed through today's common processes where people choose a design from a builder and hire contractors to piece together the finished product. The Salvias designed, fashioned, and built their home using their own creative minds and an abundance of determination.

While building their home, the Salvias lived in a mutual friend's hunting cabin. This continued for several years while they cleared their land and built their house. Throughout the years, the Salvias maintained their optimistic resolve. We watched them joyfully live in their simple conditions. The hunting cabin had running water and electricity. It was suitable for outdoorsy hunters who needed a place to stay warm and dry. However, it did not have an indoor toilet, shower, or any bedrooms. Despite this, their daughter, Summer, Laurel, and I created more fun experiences at that hunting cabin. My memories of those years are only good ones. We ran through the forest acting out whimsical adventures. We hand-washed dishes while singing at the top of our lungs. We warmed ourselves around the wood stove while playing cards. We enjoyed sleepovers in the loft. And we took cautious trips to the outhouse after dark. The simplicity and joy I found within the Salvias' makeshift home left an impression on my mind. With an enthusiastic attitude and faithful friends, life's challenges can be shaped into beautiful blessings.

I can see now that both of our parents believed this simple way of life was just a season. As with all seasons, change is inevitable. There was a positive expectation that circumstances were going to improve. We all had hope for a better future. We joyfully embraced the hard work and cultivated the world around us. We created goodness out of nature's provision.

Growing up surrounded by these kinds of people shaped my mindset about life. I watched them approach challenges with the question, "How can we do this?" Some leadership experts call this a "growth mindset." As I am facing a challenging season, I'm going back to that possibility mindset. I'm challenging my thoughts of *I can't do that* with_____ *Why not? There's got to be a way!* Those days when I keep my more positive mindset, I attribute it to my parents' grit and resourcefulness.

As an adult, I enjoy abundance. I don't apologize for living more extravagantly than I once did. At times I even forget my humble beginnings. Do you ever find yourself losing sight of your past? Does discontentment sometimes creep into your heart? How quickly we can disassociate from our previous years, especially if our current life bears little resemblance to the life we once lived. I think when we remember where we came from, we stay grateful.

Although I don't live the same simple lifestyle in which I was raised, I desire to recognize the hard work that allows my family and me to enjoy abundance. I don't have to produce everything on my own. I don't have to work as physically hard as my parents did. Yet I appreciate the endeavors of those who do. I now take joy in generously supporting the efforts of farmers, ranchers, and craftsmen. The dry, arid climate of my Colorado home requires excessive amounts of water for gardening so that's not something I've continued. Instead, I enjoy supporting local, Colorado farmers through crop sharing initiatives. I seek out resourceful people and champion their causes.

Thinking back to these days has made me reconsider the principle of sowing and reaping. We did it physically and reaped a physical harvest. Now I'm considering what else I can sow. Encouragement? Effort? Thankfulness?

As I finished writing this chapter, I challenged myself to evaluate my mindset. Maybe I've taken too much for granted. Maybe at times, I've even become ungrateful. I desire to change. To remember my past. To grow in gratitude. I'm asking myself again whether I'm being resourceful. I'm looking at each season with fresh eyes, considering its rhythms. I'm finding ways to enjoy nature's bounty — even if it's just buying what's in season in the produce aisles! It's all making gratitude bubble up within me like a lifegiving well.

I guess little actions still produce a harvest. Even when the harvest is in my heart.

Rediscovering
FAITH

Be devoted to one another in brotherly love;
give preference to one another in honor;
not lagging behind in diligence,
fervent in spirit, serving the Lord.

— Romans 12:10 (NASB1995)

I wish not merely to be called a Christian,
but also to be a Christian.

— Saint Ignatius

"What are we, Dad?" I asked one day. "Are we Baptist, Nazarene, Pentecostal...?" My voice trailed off as I listed several church denominations our family had attended. "Christians, Lizzy, we are Christians," Dad answered. "We aren't a denomination. We are followers of Christ."

My father's answer remains with me to this day. For as long as I can remember, a rhythm of faith sustained our family. Dad's family vision prioritized faith. While he was (and still is) a spontaneous character, Dad tenaciously cultivated his personal faith. His example overflowed into our family.

Throughout my growing up years, Dad initiated daily family devotions. Mom and Dad are both early birds. Most mornings started at the crack of dawn, gathered around the table. After eating breakfast, Dad pulled out his Bible. As a family, we read and memorized Scripture and then ended the time with prayer. Dad encouraged everyone to share prayer requests. We each prayed aloud.

The morning Bible readings usually consisted of a Psalm or New Testament Scripture. However, when devotions didn't occur in the morning, we gathered in the living room after supper. Evening devotions resembled story time, and everyone cuddled together on the couch. Dad read many different stories — from Joseph's leadership in Egypt to David's bravery with Goliath. However, my personal favorite was of Queen Esther saving her people. Her beauty, strength, and bravery fascinated me. I wanted to be just like her.

Just as faith opened our days, it also closed them. I enjoyed the evening routine. Once I was in bed, Dad and Mom visited my bedroom. They laid their productive, gentle hands upon me and prayed blessings over me. These special times continued throughout high school until I left home. I loved being tucked in and prayed over every night (I still do). They did that for each of us kids.

In addition to our daily rhythms of faith, we had a weekly rhythm. My parents set aside each Sunday as a day of worship and rest. For Dad and Mom, Sunday was "The Lord's Day." Every Sunday we joined other Christians at a local church.

As referenced earlier, my family didn't stick to a single denomination. We often lived in remote communities even before our years in Millinocket. While there was always a church to belong to, we just never knew which denomination would be a good fit. So, we visited different churches until settling into the one that best fit our family's faith values.

As I mentioned in Chapter One, Dad and Pastor Bob Catalano were good friends before we moved to Maine. Bob pastored Millinocket Church of the Nazarene. The Catalanos were the only people we knew in Millinocket when we arrived. Their special family welcomed us and immediately connected us to their church. The people in their church treated us like family. From the first time we attended, I thoroughly enjoyed the children's programs. I also enjoyed the music.

My family valued the artistry of music, both instrumental and lyrical. My siblings and I all learned to play the piano, and Laurel and I cultivated the skill. Mom tells me that I liked to play from the time I was about four years old. I especially liked church songs. I figured them out after coming home from Sunday service. As I grew older, I had many opportunities to play and sing at church. As I said before, I don't like to perform in front of people. Yet I do love to worship Jesus through music.

I still feel the most connected to God through music. When my kids were toddlers, I didn't frequently play the piano. I set aside my hobby for over a decade and missed it so much. Over the past year, I've started playing again. My kids can entertain themselves now, so I take advantage of little moments of respite. Joy and peace flood my heart as I sit and play my piano. God frequently touches my heart through music.

Isn't it beautiful how God speaks to you uniquely, according to the way He wired you? For example, I'm quite heart-centric. God frequently speaks to my heart. On the other hand, one of my dear friends is incredibly intellectual. God often speaks to her mind. I am thankful there are so many ways to experience God's presence.

Continuing with my church experiences in Maine, Millinocket Church of the Nazarene was special. The people in that church cared for one another. They lived out their values through their actions. Their example portrayed the love of Christ in a very tangible way. Additionally, the Nazarene Church's children's director coordinated a variety of engaging activities for kids. Her energy and enthusiasm were contagious. What I saw in my family and the church attracted me to Christianity. So, from a young age, I decided to follow Jesus.

While we started every Sunday with church, Dad and Mom initiated a rhythm of rest for the remainder of the day. They were not legalistic about the practice. They were just following the Biblical admonition to "Remember the Sabbath and keep it holy" (although I realize the Jewish Sabbath occurs on Saturday, not Sunday). Sundays were a peaceful day of rest.

We typically enjoyed a delicious meal after church. Sometimes we invited friends to join us for lunch. Other times our family just enjoyed the company of each other. Always an avid reader, I often spent Sunday afternoons with a book. During the summer months, Dad initiated family projects around the house. Picking up the backyard and gardening were common Sunday afternoon activities.

At that time, I didn't have an appreciation for the day's slower pace. However, as I've grown older, I fathom the importance of practicing "Sabbath" every week.

Our family desired to live an authentic, Christian life. So as a child, I frequently talked about my faith and invited neighborhood friends to church. Neighborhood sisters, Krystal and Kendra, lived around the corner from us. Laurel and I played with them frequently. Krystal, Laurel, and I shared the same fourth grade class. While they lived in Millinocket, Krystal and Kendra attended church with us almost every Sunday. We had so much fun together! Isn't life always more fun when shared with others? I felt the same when it came to sharing my faith. I was just sharing the joy!

However, back then I also tended to view life as very white and black. Right and wrong. Innocent or guilty. Thankfully, as I've grown older, my humility has grown as well. My father was a great example of humility. Dad adhered to the Bible but he wasn't pushy or judgmental of people who didn't practice the same beliefs as he did. When I acted judgmentally, Dad gently admonished me, saying, "Lizzy, we are not the judge of someone else's heart. It's not our job to judge. That's between them and God." I admire Dad's ability to live his faith through his actions and, only when necessary, to use words.

During our third year in Millinocket, Pastor Bob tragically contracted an inoperable brain tumor. He died shortly after his diagnosis, leaving behind his family and church. My young mind filled with questions and uncertainty. I couldn't understand why he died so young. Why his children were without their dad. Why the church lost its beloved pastor. Although my parents helped us process the situation, Pastor Bob's death was quite traumatic. Even years later, I am reminded that not all questions have easy answers. I still don't quite comprehend situations like this. Yet I now feel peace knowing I don't have to figure everything out in this life.

A couple new pastors came through the church during the interim. One soon filled Pastor Bob's position. He had many great qualities, and my parents submitted to his leadership for a time. But instead of seeking perspective from the congregation, the new leader quickly implemented his own vision for the future. He failed to consider the church's culture. Unfortunately, the hurting church fractured.

Several causes contributed to the tension. One was the teaching. Dad and Mom prioritized Biblical teaching. As they listened to the pastor's sermons, they felt concerned that some of the pastor's primary beliefs were not anchored in God's Word. Even so, they didn't make a hasty decision to leave. They cultivated understanding and built a relationship with the new leader. Still, over the following year, the messages continued to deviate from their understanding of the Bible. So, Mom and Dad decided to move on.

During this time, Laurel and I were toward the end of our middle school years. Due to the conflict and culture changes at church, we both lost our enjoyment of faith-filled gatherings. Thankfully, Dad and Mom noticed the environment's negative impact on us. That factor also influenced their decision to switch churches.

While many families today may not see the need for corporate church gatherings, Dad and Mom recognized the value of a positive association for their kids. Especially for Laurel and me. We lacked close friends. Looking back, my parents could have fostered faith exclusively within the walls of our home. They already had positive disciplines in place. Staying home probably would have been easier instead of searching for a new church. However, they set aside their convenience in order to fulfill their kids' needs for wholesome friendships.

The remote towns of Maine don't have many churches to choose from. There were several other good options in Millinocket, but my parents kept searching the surrounding area. Through a referral from Dad's local friend, Herschel Hafford, we discovered Community Evangel Temple. For the next four years, we attended that church.

Community Evangel Temple, also known as CET, is a small church in Lincoln, Maine. Lincoln is one of the towns surrounding Millinocket. Even so, it's 40 miles away. The teaching, the discipleship, and the youth group were just what we needed during that time. Pastor Shaw welcomed our family with open arms. He passionately educated the congregation and taught directly from the Bible. I really enjoyed his teaching and learned so much from him. The music was great too! Youth Pastor Jason Johnstone led the congregation in many lively and worshipful songs. My passion for Jesus started to reignite once more.

CET's youth group impacted me the most! On our first Sunday, a sweet young woman named Michelle introduced herself. Similar in age to Laurel and me, Michelle was beautiful inside and out. She was tall and slender, and her blonde, curly hair cascaded down her back. Her green eyes sparkled with joy. Michelle looked like a model. I later discovered she was one! Michelle participated in beauty pageants and even won Miss Maine National Teen-Ager. She was articulate and a community leader. Most importantly, Michelle exuded the warmth and love of Jesus. She immediately embraced Laurel and me and made us feel right at home. When she invited us to Wednesday night youth group, we eagerly accepted.

Over the next several years, Michelle became a dear friend. Even following our time at CET, Michelle's friendship ministered to my heart. I later invited her to be a bridesmaid in my wedding, and she accepted. I treasure Michelle's friendship to this day!

The youth pastor and his wife, Jason and Sue Johnstone, along with their assistants, Benny and Carol, were incredible role models of God's joy, peace, and love. Although Pastor Jason and Sue were quite young, they effectively discipled us in our faith. All four adults were instrumental in helping Laurel and me deepen our personal relationship with God.

They also coordinated exciting activities for the youth group! Laurel and I participated in as many outings as Mom and Dad allowed. We went white water rafting, water skiing, and downhill skiing. Involvement in CET's youth group proved a Christian's life didn't have to be dull or boring. One ski trip was especially memorable. The youth group bus broke down on our way home from Sunday River! Benny, who drove the bus, creatively fixed the engine problem with duct tape. Who knew duct tape could be so useful?

Throughout our years at CET, Laurel and I once again developed a passion to share our faith with our friends. Every Sunday and Wednesday, we packed our eight-passenger van to above capacity! Truthfully, I despised that two-toned tan and brown vehicle. It was beyond ugly. Yet its size served our family and guests well. We added friends by setting up lawn chairs in the very back of the van! The chairs were flimsy, so friends had to stabilize themselves when Dad drove around corners! We made many boisterous caravans to and from Lincoln. Those rides were far from luxury. And probably not very safe. But many neighborhood friends talk about the impact those trips had on their lives.

Toward the end of my junior year, Dad decided to change churches again. His friend, Herschel, had a vision for the communities of Millinocket and East Millinocket. He spearheaded a non-denominational church and community outreach called I Care Ministries (ICM). Herschel is the same friend who initially referred us to CET. Dad always believed in fostering the local community. So, when Herschel started ICM, Dad loyally supported his efforts.

Herschel established I Care Ministries in an old armory. Conveniently built in the very center of Millinocket, the armory was only one mile away from our home. Laurel and I exchanged tearful goodbyes with our friends at CET. We still connected with the youth group for seasonal outings, but we once again plugged into Millinocket's church community.

In all honesty, I initially resented my parents for their decision. I didn't want to like the new church. The music was lacking, the facility was rundown, and the teaching was different from what I was accustomed to. I think others felt the same. But Dad gently coached all of us on the importance of supporting Herschel's efforts. Dad believed in Herschel's vision.

Over time, I decided to change my attitude and get involved. Laurel and I started co-leading worship with a dear woman named Mary. Mary exuded enthusiasm, and her joy was contagious! We sang and played the piano together every week. Mary also hosted a Bible study for the youth. The church had humble beginnings, and the congregation was small. But I grew to love our time there. I felt thankful for my parents' commitment to Herschel.

I now admire Herschel. His vision for the community was God-sized. He obediently stepped out to follow the calling he felt for the town. Herschel started a food bank, initiated teen programs, and mentored local families. Years later, he started Katahdin Christian Academy, a private school dedicated to cultivating a strong culture of faith and education.

I am forever thankful for all three Maine churches, especially for the people. Each shaped me into who I am today. Although Pastor Bob passed before I could personally thank him, I am so grateful for his influence. Not only did he lead well as a pastor, but it was because of his encouragement that prompted our family's move to Maine! What an amazing impact one person can have on others' lives.

During a recent visit to Maine, I visited the Johnstones and the Haffords. It had been twenty years since I saw the Johnstones, and a decade for the Haffords. Both reunions were remarkable. My heart overflowed with gratitude for these incredible people. Jason and Sue Johnstone are now the senior pastors of CET. And Herschel is still serving I Care Ministries, Katahdin Christian Academy, and other community projects. His heart for Millinocket and East Millinocket is larger than ever.

Growing up in a faith-filled family taught me many things. First of all, experiencing faith within my home impacted me more than any corporate church ever did. Dad and Mom modeled the simplicity of the Christian life in real, authentic ways. My parents' relationship with me reflected gentleness, blessing, and grace. Their example helped me better understand God's heart of grace.

Dad's commitment to the daily disciplines of prayer and Bible reading positively impacted the whole family. I talked a lot about that in this chapter, maybe because I believe those times instilled security, unity, and love into our family. Yet my Mom's faith is also incredible. Her life reminds me of the beautiful growth journey that we all can experience if we remain humble and teachable. I admire Mom's hunger to grow spiritually. I rarely see this quality in people her age. She's enthusiastic about learning and dedicated to discipleship. She's grown in grace, blossomed in patience, and demonstrated faithfulness. Mom is an inspiration to me. I love the way she is intentional about growing.

Neither Mom nor Dad take credit for our decisions to follow Christ. But I believe each of us kids embraced a lifestyle of faith because of their incredible example.

Mom frequently read stories about Jesus caring for the children, healing the sick, and loving the unlovely. Starting at a young age, my sensitive heart wanted a friendship with Jesus, the God who was so kind and compassionate.

The Bible says, "Everyone who calls on the name of the Lord will be saved." My childlike heart accepted this promise as Truth. I didn't pray a complicated prayer or recite a long list of sins that needed forgiveness. My relationship with Jesus started as a simple act of faith. Despite the simplicity, my decision was heartfelt and real. I knew beyond a shadow of a doubt that I was a part of God's family.

As I continued my faith journey throughout my youth and into adulthood, the beautiful simplicity of God's grace hasn't ever become old. Instead, it's become more and more vibrant! I remain forever grateful to Dad and Mom for stressing the simplicity of following Jesus.

Do these stories bring back any faith connections from your youth that need repair? Maybe it wasn't your family but friends who cultivated faith or brought you to church. Did you like those practices and experience God's grace and peace? Or do you have a past hurtful experience with the church that needs to be forgiven for your own freedom?

It is here that I would like to pause and offer empathy. So many have been hurt by people who claim to be Christians. If you've been hurt, I just want to say that I am so, so sorry. My prayer for you is that you would not reject Christ due to the negligence of Christians. I recently listened to a podcast where Andy Stanley interviewed author, historian, and professor, Dr. John Dickson. Dr. Dickson shares thoughts from his book, *Has Christianity Done More Harm than Good?* The book explores the history of Christianity and reviews the good and the bad throughout the last two millennia as a result of the Christian faith.

Darkness lurks in the corners of history. At times it threatens to overshadow the beautiful light of God's love and grace. However, Dr. Dickson concludes his research by offering a powerful analogy for listeners to consider. He relates Christianity to Johanne Sebastian Bach's Cello Suites. Classical and contemporary musicians alike appreciate and admire this piece. It's arguably one of the most intricate masterpieces ever composed. Dr. Dickson asks listeners to consider the tunes of two different performers. Listeners good-naturedly laugh at Dr. Dickson's humble attempts and then marvel when a professional performs the piece. Dr. Dickson then continues to compare and contrast Christianity to the differences between the two.

Dr. Dickson admits that at times Christians have done a poor job. He acknowledges that the distorted music of Christianity has been humanity's amateur attempts to play the divine song. Despite this, he concludes that the melody of Christ is still beautiful. He encourages listeners to receive Christ despite Christians' poor performance. No matter what, Christ's Gospel is still a masterpiece. He loved His enemies, He did good to those who persecuted Him, and He extended His grace and mercy to all people.

My family and I have been hurt by many people who call themselves Christians. I'll sadly admit I've hurt people as well. However, I am thankful that despite my failures to perfectly live out my faith, there is One who remains Faithful through it all. So, if you've been hurt by Christians, would you consider allowing Christ to heal your scarred places as only He can?

Another lesson I learned is to focus on what unites and not on what divides. My family focused on following Christ, not denominational doctrine. I experienced the beautiful aspects of God and the life of faith within each church we attended. Obviously, I shared from my participation within the Protestant church. However, I have many friends who practice Catholicism, and I respect their faith journeys as well. We are all unique, and I think that denominations just reflect that uniqueness. I've come to ask myself, *Does my faith walk stem out of my relationship with Jesus and His love for people, or am I just adhering to religious practices?* My hope is the former, not the latter.

My last thought is on the value of observing the Sabbath. As I reflected on my upbringing, I contrasted it to my current life. I realized that I've strayed from "remembering the Sabbath and keeping it holy." I've maintained the habit of weekly church attendance. But Sundays have become just another day. Somewhere along the way, I stopped setting aside Sundays for rest and worship. It became an extension of my already overcommitted week.

These past years, I inadvertently allowed weekly responsibilities to continue non-stop, day after day, week after week, year after year — until I finally broke. I think it's been close to a decade since heeding the Biblical practice of rest.

As I remembered my own stories, I wondered if my frenetic pace played a part in my breaking. I think so. And this was after watching many friends experience adrenal fatigue, emotional breakdowns, and burnout. Why did I think I was immune to the very same destruction?

Are you where I have been — on the verge of breaking — physically, emotionally, and mentally? Lately, I've been rediscovering that a rhythm of rest was instituted from the beginning of Creation. Genesis 2:2–3 says, "By the seventh day God had finished the work He had been doing; so on the seventh day He rested from all His work. Then God blessed the seventh day and made it holy, because on it He rested from all the work of creating that He had done." I don't think God rested because He was tired from His work. I think He sat back, beheld the heavens and earth, and rejoiced! Creation was magnificent! I think God delighted in the beauty that surrounded Him. What an incredible example for us to follow.

I just recently introduced the Sabbath into my weekly rhythm once again. My family and I set aside a day to stop and delight in all that is good, beautiful, and lovely. Already anxiety and dread are diminishing.

I've also discovered that whether my rest day occurs on Saturday or Sunday is not the point. It seems to be more about stopping to enjoy and appreciate — and rest. Jesus once told a lawyer of his day, "The Sabbath was made for man, not man for the Sabbath." I'm choosing that perspective of it. This once-a-week rhythm seems to recalibrate our spirits and souls into a restful rhythm.

These rest days remind me of Jesus's invitation, "Come to me all you who are weary and burdened, and I will give you rest." (Matthew 11:28) Giving me rest? I'm in. Want to join me?

Rediscovering
INNOVATION

Whatever you do, work at it with all your heart,
as working for the Lord, not for human masters…
it is the Lord Christ you are serving.

— Colossians 3:23–24 (NIV)

Failure is success in progress.

— Albert Einstein

An innovative atmosphere permeated our home. Mom initiated alternative education, and Dad embraced entrepreneurship. These two areas greatly influenced my mindset and ambition.

Early on, Mom decided to homeschool. She initially started when we lived in New York. Challenges with the nearby public schools influenced her decision. Mom discovered a fulfilling enjoyment as she educated her own children. I really liked it too. As I mentioned earlier, Laurel and I attended public school during our first year in Maine. It was a good experience and worked well while Mom and Dad finished remodeling our home. We truly enjoyed fourth grade at Katahdin Elementary School. However, we also really appreciated many aspects of homeschooling, so Mom decided to homeschool us again starting in fifth grade.

At that time homeschooling was not commonplace. Even so, Mom continued with her resolution for several reasons. First, Mom loved learning and enjoyed teaching. She recognized the value in individualized learning plans. Mom also valued family time. She wanted us siblings to be great friends. She thought she could cultivate sibling friendships if we spent more time together. Lastly, Mom wanted to be our primary influencer. She maintained strong values and desired to pass these on. Mom's commitment was not easy, and I admire her resolve. Especially during a time when the practice was just launching.

Our school days were disciplined yet flexible. Mom focused on life skills as well as academics. Accountability, work ethic, and time management were just as important as math, grammar, and writing. Expectations were high. We rose early, making our beds neat and tidy. Even as a young girl, my brain efficiently organized tasks. During the temperate months, I slept atop my quilt so I didn't have to remake my bed daily. However, this habit didn't work quite as well during the cold winters!

Mom also expected us to get dressed and look presentable. She allowed us flexibility with our wardrobe, but pajamas weren't a daytime option. Mom prioritized routine as if we attended a conventional school. We consistently worked through our lessons at the kitchen table, and we usually finished our schoolwork by noon.

Mom's discipline and patience amaze me. She calmly worked with each of us until we obtained mastery. Sometimes Laurel and I helped Amber and Seth with their subjects. Other times we worked independently. As Mom hoped, the time around the table did foster friendship among us. We all share a special closeness to this day.

Laurel and I were goal-oriented and independent. We frequently worked together and ambitiously completed our school work quickly. My favorite subjects included language arts, reading, and writing. I often completed multiple lessons each day, working ahead at my own pace. I enjoyed the flexibility and independence. I still do.

Mom thoughtfully considered the strengths and weaknesses of her children. I've always been an achiever. I like to maintain control and complete things perfectly. I expect myself to master activities quickly even if I've never done them before. As I've matured, I've realized that control is an illusion and perfection is unattainable. I *can* control my attitude toward myself, others, and situations. But I *cannot* control people or circumstances around me. Similarly, I can work on tasks with excellence. However, my best may still fall short. As a child, my desire for control and perfection produced frustration and anxiety. Sometimes it still does. Mom strategically navigated my shortcomings as they arose.

I had different challenges each year. However, two instances stick out in my mind. Mom patiently navigated both. The first instance occurred in third grade. I had just started cursive writing. Although I've always loved to write, the strokes and curves of handwriting were so challenging. I shed many frustrated tears as I attempted to duplicate the beautiful letters I saw in my workbook. I expected mastery would come rapidly and felt like a failure when it didn't. Frustration overwhelmed my ability to progress.

Similar frustrations occurred in eighth grade with algebra. Our math curriculum was always quite advanced, and the complex concepts we learned that year challenged my young mind. Once again, I despised my inability to understand quickly. I felt inadequate and incapable. On many mornings, I succumbed to tears. However, Mom valued mastery, not just completion. So, she gently set aside the curriculum that year and focused on other mathematical skills. She focused on what I *could* do. Mom fostered a love for learning, and that objective trumped the goal of finishing the curriculum. Student-centered in her approach, Mom didn't expect us to serve the curriculum. The curriculum was there to serve us.

In case you are wondering, I eventually mastered both cursive writing and algebra. Today, I find incredible enjoyment in writing "old-fashioned" notes to the people I love. I almost always write these notes in cursive. Additionally, when I took algebra for the second time in tenth grade, I passed the class with honors. Ironically, I took multiple math classes in college and thoroughly enjoyed them. I'm not sure I would have pursued any additional math if Mom forced algebra before I was ready.

In addition to academics, Mom cultivated life skills. She thought these were just as important as education. Mom is one of the most capable women I know. She finishes more tasks in a day than most people finish in a week. Yet she didn't complete all of the home responsibilities on her own. Instead, Mom taught us the value of working together. She reiterated over and over, "We are a family, and families help each other out."

Mom strategically assigned daily responsibilities. It seems as though most chores occurred in the kitchen (and still do). It became a place of activity after mealtimes! Mom gave Laurel and me the task of washing dishes. As I mentioned before, we did not have a dishwasher and washed all of our dishes by hand. Contrary to what you might think, it was actually quite fun! Laurel and I turned on our boombox and blared our favorite music as loud as Mom could tolerate.

Why did Mom give Laurel and me this chore? Well, when we tried doing dishes with our younger sister, Helene, it never ended well! Up until my senior year of high school, Laurel and I didn't get along with Helene at all. We all like to be in charge. Of the three of us, Helene has the strongest personality. I never liked being bossed around, especially by my younger sister. Laurel and I frequently reminded Helene of her place. Many verbal eruptions ensued due to the sibling rivalry.

Instead of berating us for fighting with our younger sister, Mom figured out which personalities worked best together. She assigned partners accordingly. Sometime later, I realized that Mom had figured out a key principle in getting along with people. While everyone deserves honor and respect, there will be some people you get along with and others you don't. And that's okay. Thankfully, Mom understood our family's dynamics and didn't force what didn't work. Needless to say, all it took was time and maturity. Helene is one of my best friends today!

Helene swept the kitchen floor after every meal (no robotic vacuums in those days). Amber and Seth? Well, we joke that they enjoyed the benefits of being the youngest children and inadvertently shirked most duties around the house! At least during our years in Maine!

Chores didn't only happen around mealtimes but occurred throughout the week as well. With a family of seven, we had a lot of laundry! Even with the laundry, Mom implemented a disciplined system that involved us kids. Mom woke us up at 7 a.m. every morning as she collected our clothes. "Time to rise and shine," she cheerfully announced. At the time I grumbled at the wake-up calls, nor did I enjoy folding and putting away the laundry later in the day. However, I now admire Mom's energy and discipline, even in the midst of mundane tasks.

Because Mom encouraged family participation around the house, I developed an enjoyment of several household responsibilities. Cooking and baking quickly became favorites. Because of our love for creating in the kitchen, Mom allowed Laurel and me to fix lunch. We often cooked supper as well. Mom taught us everything she knew about baking and cooking. She gave us grace when we made mistakes and always encouraged our creativity.

Saturday mornings also involved chores. We did not sleep in or watch cartoons. Instead, Mom initiated a thorough house cleaning. Homeschool work and other responsibilities trumped house cleaning during the week, but order and cleanliness were priorities for Mom. Without fail, Mom made out her cleaning list every Saturday. She still always has some type of list going. The Saturday list always included the bathroom, dusting, washing the floors, organizing bedrooms, and putting away accumulated clutter.

At times we voiced our opinions about Saturday morning chores. "All the other kids in the neighborhood don't have to clean their houses on Saturday morning, so why do we?" Our complaints were ineffective. Mom replied, "You aren't all the other kids. You are *my* kids, and we work together until the job is done." We quickly changed our tune and worked as hard and as fast as we could. As soon as we finished cleaning the house, we enjoyed the reward of playtime.

These routines taught me the value of cultivating an environment of discipline. Daily chores and weekend organizing times imprinted a strong work ethic upon my heart. I also discovered that discipline is needed to keep life running in an orderly fashion. I guess it was Mom's way of quietly teaching us that life's positive trajectory doesn't just happen. It takes thoughtful intentionality and daily discipline. I am so grateful Mom instilled these values in us.

While Mom was the epitome of education and discipline, Dad embodied entrepreneurship and creativity. Watching my dad live outside the lines prompted me to do the same. One way Laurel and I expressed our creativity was through writing plays. While we did not ever perform these plays on stage, we did create costumes to outfit our characters. One time Laurel and I designed and sewed blouses. Without a pattern. Mom didn't deviate from instructions, so she felt quite concerned about our endeavor. She recommended a pattern. However, Laurel and I had a mental picture of what the blouses should look like. The pattern didn't fit what we had in our heads so we moved forward without it.

Mom patiently equipped us with fabric, her sewing machine, and other tools we needed. Laurel and I worked diligently on the blouses. After we finished, we realized that some of our measurements were a bit off. Truthfully, we didn't do any measurements. We had only visualized the finished product. Those tops were not very useful. They didn't fit! At all.

Thankfully Mom didn't brag about being right nor did she put us down for being stubborn. She instead suggested that next time we find and modify a similar pattern. Perhaps we might mitigate some of our challenges with fit? We heeded her advice years later when we decided to sew our prom dresses. We envisioned what we wanted, but this time we realized that we could modify patterns to create them. Failure taught me that having a blueprint can save time and money. I think flexibility within the plan is key.

What have you learned from your creative failures? Do you tend to pursue creativity at the risk of failure or stick to a plan at the expense of creativity? Can you find value in both?

Watching Dad with his businesses fostered a curiosity for entrepreneurship. I felt excited to try new things. As I mentioned earlier, Laurel and I dreamed of owning a horse. Instead of brushing off that desire, both parents encouraged us to formulate plans to achieve that goal. At the age of 10, we figured out the annual cost of keeping a horse. Then we developed plans for a pet-caring business and presented them to our parents. Once they approved, we wrote an ad for the Katahdin Times newspaper and networked with the community to get clients. These efforts birthed our pet-caring business and the initial funds for our horse. It was a great source of income for many years.

While most of our jobs were fun and uneventful, many interesting situations occurred throughout our years of service. One time we cared for a parakeet. We knew the family from church. The lady of the house was from the Philippines, so the family vacationed there every summer. We cared for their houseplants and their bird while they were away. We visited their house weekly to care for the plants, but their parakeet stayed at our house in Helene and Amber's room. Although it had a cage, my sisters often removed the colorful bird from its cage and allowed it to fly around their room.

Even though Maine's weather remains moderately temperate throughout the summer, the upstairs of our small home collected heat. To maintain airflow, we opened windows and enjoyed the cool, outdoor breeze. While most of our windows had screens, Helene and Amber's room did not. Mom warned them to keep their window shut during the parakeet's stay. One day they forgot. The parakeet took full advantage of his opportunity for escape, flew out the window, and landed on the tree in our front yard.

Helene and Amber immediately panicked! The bird was gone! They frantically sought out Mom. She set aside her plans for the afternoon and together they hunted down the bird. Laurel and I weren't home, otherwise we would have joined in the rescue. Around and around the neighborhood they went, following the bird from tree to tree. Their efforts were to no avail. The parakeet escaped, and he never came back.

Mom required Helene to take responsibility for the situation, so Helene used her personal funds to purchase our clients a new bird. She also had to inform them of the mishap. When the family returned, we presented the new parakeet and apologetically informed them of the situation. Much to our surprise, they laughed at the predicament. "We weren't fond of the parakeet anyway," they said. "You shouldn't have purchased us another bird. We would have been satisfied without a new one."

I could share so many more memories of our pet-caring business. It was such a great real-world experience for us. Over the years, we cared for dozens of dogs. We watched multiple horses. There were times when animals got into mischief or escaped their pens. I found that more mishaps occurred when I stretched myself too thin. Excellence was compromised. Learning how to prioritize one thing at a time has been an ongoing lesson for me.

One comical memory of stretching myself too thin ironically involved expanding bread dough. During my high school years, I not only ran my pet business and maintained other jobs but also baked pastries, pies, and cinnamon rolls for a local coffee shop. The shop owner, affectionately nicknamed "Ninee," initially asked Dad to bake goodies for her business. He would periodically make fruit-filled turnovers and Danish. Due to his busy schedule, he later delegated this task to Laurel and me. We loved fulfilling Ninee's orders! While imparting his culinary wisdom, Dad frequently reminded us that baked goods need constant attention. "Keep your eye on the dough," he would warn.

Despite his admonition, we still tried to juggle too many tasks at the same time.

One beautiful summer day, we received an order. Ninee wanted cinnamon rolls for the next morning. We agreed and started the process. These treats are so delicious to eat yet incredibly time-consuming to make. First, you knead the dough. Next, you let it rise. This rising process is called "proofing." It's important to allow yeast breads the proper amount of time to proof. When done correctly, proofing activates the yeast. The fermentation between the yeast, starches, and gluten gives bread its pliable, yet pillowy, structure. After its first rise, you roll out the dough and layer it with generous portions of butter, cinnamon, sugar, and raisins. Then you cut and place the rolls into their pans, allowing them to proof for a second time. Finally, you bake the rolls, let them cool, and slather them with icing. From start to finish, the rolls can take many hours.

For this order, Laurel and I figured we would complete the first step and leave for another activity while the dough proofed. As I mentioned, the weather was warm and sunny. Our enclosed front porch collected the heat and was a perfect spot to expedite the proofing process. After we kneaded the dough, we set our oversized mixing bowl on the porch and set off for our next venture.

Yeast breads can take an hour or more to double in size. However, temperature dramatically affects the proofing rate. The warmth of the porch efficiently activated the yeast, and the scrumptious dough proliferated. Abundantly. By the time we returned, the bread dough had more than doubled

— it had multiplied! It didn't just expand above the rim of the bowl but had climbed over the rim, down the side of the bowl, and made its way onto the floor. Laurel and I had to discard the entire batch of dough and start all over again. The tedious task became elongated due to our lack of focus.

Throughout high school, Laurel and I worked many different jobs. We held jobs at Big Moose Inn Cabin and Campgrounds, Twin Pines, River Drivers, and Kelley Mobile Home Park. I loved working and discovered great joy in the accomplishment of a job well done. Lines between play and work often became blurred. They still do. During these years, I started learning about the differences between employment and business ownership. Compensation from employment was more consistent than running my own business. However, I liked the flexibility of my business, choosing when to work and which clients to accept. I loved the variety of work back then. I still value variety today, preferring to diversify between the consistency of employment and the creativity of entrepreneurship.

I am now a mom. The weight of responsibility I feel for my four kids is indescribable. Cultivating an atmosphere of learning and curiosity is something I aspire to do. Are these facets important to you? I am sure they are. Yet as I look around, I feel concerned. I frequently see safety and security prioritized at the expense of curiosity and creativity. Does this concern you too?

When you admire the innovators from centuries past, do you stop and ask yourself how they were able to achieve their accomplishments? Were they given the freedom to pursue a goal-and the freedom to fail? I think so. As a child,

I failed frequently. As I mentioned, I never liked failure. I still don't. Interestingly, my parents didn't label challenges as failure. They also didn't bail me out when I failed. They viewed failures as opportunities to explore and learn. I think this perspective created confidence in my siblings and me. Of course we made many mistakes. Yet we discovered that we could ultimately figure out solutions. I think this helped me develop strength and capacity.

At the time of this writing, I work in education and business. I serve as the director of a microschool, manage a statewide entrepreneurial market for children, and operate a personal commerce business. The microschool empowers kids to cultivate academic and life skills through hands-on projects, individualized instruction, and character development. My kids have really benefited from the program, and I feel privileged to run it. The school embraces multi-age classrooms, so siblings are often able to learn side by side. I feel so thankful my children can develop friendships with each other, and that other siblings can do the same. I've watched the student-centered approach cultivate creativity and a love for learning. When it comes to education, what suits your child? What develops their strengths and helps them explore?

The entrepreneurial endeavors provide opportunities for my kids and I to experience the risks and rewards of real-world business. I still enjoy the flexibility of business ownership and strive to add value to my clients on and off the web. My kids are learning alongside me to set goals and solve problems. They are also developing products to sell in order to meet their goals. Whether or not your kids participate in alternative education or are actively involved in an entrepreneurship program, you can allow them opportunities to experience business. Real-world success and failure. They can earn their desire, as we did. They could explore Junior Achievement. You could discuss with them, "How could you earn the money for that?" Then brainstorm solutions with them. Allow them to innovate, to develop discipline, all while maintaining flexibility.

I think my parents' mindset greatly influenced me. They impacted my education and empowered me in so many other ways — to set goals, and to creatively accomplish those goals. They allowed me to fail and encouraged me to learn from my failures. They undergirded me as I tried new things. They cultivated discipline and work ethic.

I've discovered through my journey that high achievers come from all different backgrounds. What strengths do you currently have that you learned from your parents or guardians? Alongside those strengths, have you discovered any weaknesses?

My growing up years cultivated creativity, efficiency, and productivity. However, through writing and reflecting, I realized that my drive presents some challenges as well. I watched my parents work incredibly hard. They modeled high capacities. Both frequently say, "Yes!" "Yes," to people and "Yes," to opportunities. I am truly grateful for their example. I've developed similar behaviors. I work hard and maintain a high capacity. Yet I've realized that every time I say "Yes" to a person or opportunity, I am unintentionally saying "No" to someone or something else. Often at the expense of my family. I end up spreading myself too thin, becoming overcommitted, and trying to focus on many good things at the same time. Too many things. And like the failed cinnamon rolls, my lack of focus sometimes hinders efficiency and dilutes excellence.

I realized that I learned to accomplish, but at the cost of adding margin. As a kid, I maximized my study time so I could get to my fun faster. But over the years, what started as goal setting and getting to fun became squeezing too much in. I was accomplishing but without the reward of rhythm, of family time, of friends, and of just enjoying my life. I'm beginning to redefine how I maximize my moments. In the introduction of this book, I wrote about my kitchen moment. Spinning too many plates at the expense of my family, my health, and, ultimately, my sanity. I enjoy innovation, goal-setting, and accomplishment! Now I'm also learning the value of slowing down enough to enjoy the day, the hour, even the minute before me.

As I look ahead toward this next year, I'm still juggling more than one venture. I'm still passionate about progressive education and entrepreneurial endeavors. I embrace discipline, goal setting, and innovation. Yet in the midst of these, I'm learning to add margin, to breathe, and to just enjoy life's moments. I am slowly narrowing my focus. Trimming away the excess. And learning how to say no so I can say yes to what truly matters.

On that note, it's time to go play with my kids. I'll join you again soon.

Rediscovering
ADVENTURE

O Lord, our Lord, how majestic is your name
in all the earth!
You have displayed Your splendor
above the heavens!

— Psalm 8:1 (NASB1995)

God writes the Gospel not in the Bible alone,
but also in trees, and in the flowers
and clouds and stars.

— Martin Luther

CHAPTER EIGHT

My first trip to a movie theater didn't occur until I was a junior in high school. I rarely went shopping, and we seldom ate at restaurants. So what did we do for fun? My parents, and many other Millinocket residents, embraced a simple way of life. We enjoyed God's creative outdoor playground for our fun. Time outdoors instilled peace and wonder. It was pure joy for me.

Millinocket is nestled close to the south entrance of Baxter State Park. The park boasts Mt. Katahdin and the end of the Appalachian Trail. The closest "city" is Bangor. Compared to most cities, Bangor is quite quaint and has a population around 32,000. It is 70 miles south of Millinocket and offers modern conveniences such as movie theaters, shopping, and restaurants. Some might consider the relaxed, backwoods way of life unacceptable and inconvenient. On the contrary, I loved every minute of it! I never felt as though I was missing out. In this chapter, I will share my favorite spring, summer, and fall outdoor memories. Because winter is the longest season of each year, I will devote a single chapter to those activities.

Spring blossomed slowly as the severe winter finally came to a close with daytime temperatures finally climbing above freezing. "The Thaw" began in late March or early April, melting towering snow banks and bringing an abundance of mud. Thick layers of ice dissipated from the roads. We started seeing pockets of pavement once more. Foliage and buds didn't make an appearance until closer to May. As spring progressed, the community started becoming more active.

The spring outing I most fondly remember is a fishing activity called "smelting." Smelt are minnow-sized fish that reside in estuaries and offshore waters throughout the North. These tiny fish enter streams and rivers to spawn in mid to late April. The smelt run occurs for a short period of two weeks and happens once the water temperature rises into the upper 40s. Smelt are light sensitive, so most smelt fishing occurs at night. Imagine fishing in the dark! For our early-to-bed family, this made the outing even more memorable.

News travels quickly around Millinocket. It only took a single person to announce, "The smelt are running!" Within several days, the sleepy town came alive! Our family jumped right into this annual tradition. Dad loaded his pickup truck with buckets, nets, flashlights, and other supplies. Mom made sure each of us was outfitted in warm clothes since the evening temperatures were still fairly brisk. We layered ourselves with boots, coats, hats, and mittens. Then we made the trek into the wilderness.

It was always a bumpy ride! Dirt logging roads gave access to springtime streams. The snow melt created treacherous potholes on these roads. As if that rugged ride weren't enough, we then drove off the roads to get as close to the rivers as possible. Dad's truck bounced aggressively over rocks and roots. Branches scraped each side of his vehicle. Squished in the backseat, my siblings and I desperately hung on to each other as we tried to maintain stability. After arriving at our destination, we unscrambled ourselves and prepared to fish.

Truck headlights and flashlights illuminated the springtime woods as the community enjoyed the sport together. There was a lot of excitement and boisterous activity all around the river. Mom and Dad instructed us to stay together. Dad blazed the trail. He was dressed in chest-high waders, knee-high rubber boots, and a wide-brimmed wool hat. Dad has always been a large man, but he moves quietly and quickly through the woods. It takes two or three of my strides to match one of his. Hiking to the river, we struggled to keep his pace. Especially carrying gear. Mom, Laurel, and I handled the flashlights, a five-gallon bucket, and the net.

When we finally made it to the bank of the river, Dad instructed us to stay away from the edge. The rushing river was swollen with ice and snow. The atmosphere felt almost ominous in the darkness of the night. We planted our feet securely into the muddy earth and eagerly watched our father climb down the riverbank. Like most smelt fisherman, Dad waded into the water to fish with his net.

Smelting nets are unique. The mesh net is suspended from an eight-foot aluminum handle, making it suitable for catching small, squirming fish. Dad waded into the raging current. He paid careful attention to his footing to prevent slipping into the frigid water. After he firmly planted himself, Dad collected the smelt. Slow and steady, he strongly stroked his net through the water. We excitedly awaited the net's exit. Would it contain silvery fish? Most often it did. Dad continued his strokes until we caught our daily limit. Smelt limits vary due to the amount of people in the party. Because we had seven members in our family, we harvested many quarts of the little fish!

After reaching our limit, we trekked back to Dad's truck. This time Dad carried the five-gallon bucket, now heavy with squirming smelt. Once again, we squished into one another and braced each other during the bumpy ride back to town. Even though it was always quite late when we arrived home, we immediately enjoyed some of our catch. Dad quickly cleaned, breaded, and fried the little fish. Mom made homemade tartar sauce out of mayonnaise and homemade dill pickles. Fried smelt provided crunchy goodness that is difficult to describe!

We made that trip several times over the next few weeks. We had to wait a whole year before "smelting" again. It was always worth the wait.

As spring turned into summer, Dad's guiding business moved into its busiest time of year. Mom conducted most of the family's summertime activities without my father.

As mentioned earlier, we lived only thirty minutes away from Baxter State Park. Consistent with most locations surrounding Millinocket, Baxter State Park is remote and heavily forested. A family friend named Debbie introduced us to Baxter State Park several years after we moved to Millinocket. Debbie and her boys also homeschooled. They adventurously explored the trails in the park. Debbie warmly invited our family to participate in their excursions and shared her hiking knowledge with Mom. Athletic and determined, Mom eagerly embraced hiking. Even when Debbie and her boys were not available, Mom took us on many hikes every year. She courageously included all five of us kids, starting when my younger brother, Seth, was only four.

Baxter State Park has abundant water and greenery. Because of this, black flies and mosquitoes are usually in full force. On hiking days, Mom encouraged us to wear long sleeves and pants. She wanted to protect our bare skin from the trees' scratches, and mitigate the effects of aggressive little bugs. Despite Mom's efforts, we inevitably returned home with liberal amounts of scratches and bug bites!

While we hiked multiple mountains and trails within the park, our favorite hike was Mount Katahdin. Marking the end of the Appalachian Trail (or the beginning, depending on which way you hike it), the granite peak of Mount Katahdin rises majestically above the green forest. It stands alone, boasting its lofty height of 5,269 feet. Various single-track trails weave their way up and down the mountain. Blue and white blazes mark trees and granite rocks. Appalachian Trail blazes are white. All the other trail blazes are blue. These markings are vertical rectangles about the size of a cell phone. Placed every hundred yards or so, these blazes act as a trail map and encourage hikers to stay on the trails.

Mt. Katahdin has two distinct peaks, Baxter Peak and Pamola Peak. Baxter Peak is the taller of the two and the end of the Appalachian Trail. The treacherous Knife Edge trail connects the two peaks. Several routes lead to the peaks of Mt. Katahdin. For those summiting Baxter Peak, the most direct route is called the Cathedral Trail. Not surprisingly, it is also the steepest.

To access the Cathedral Trail, hikers enjoy a relatively relaxing three mile walk to Chimney Pond. The views at Chimney Pond are magnificent. Contrary to its name, Chimney Pond is not a pond — it's a breathtaking mountain lake! Imagine a basin with rugged granite cliffs shooting toward the sky, and this is what Chimney Pond looks like. Even on cloudy days, the waters of the lake sparkle as clear as diamonds. From Chimney Pond, hikers can access trails for both Pamola Peak and Baxter Peak. Rising above the crystal-clear water, the Cathedral Trail challenges hikers from the start. It contains a towering granite boulder field. Already demanding when the weather is clear, the trail becomes more treacherous on rainy days. My most memorable Mt. Katahdin hike occurred on Cathedral Trail.

One cold, rainy day, Mom, Laurel, and I joined a group of homeschoolers for a hike. Despite the rain, we decided to summit the mountain. Our hike to Chimney Pond was uneventful. In middle school at that time, I chatted jovially with my friends while we walked. Once we reached the lake, our group stopped for a brief snack. We debated about which route to take to the summit. Our spirits were high, so we optimistically chose the Cathedral Trail.

Our group's morale changed quickly as we started our ascent. Everyone became quiet and contemplative. Because of the rain, the granite rocks were slick and cold. I was hiking toward the back of the group and wasn't moving fast enough to stay warm. My fingers soon became numb. With each step, I pulled myself onto a boulder, stabilized, re-evaluated my path, and then repeated the action. Mom's comforting presence was close by, yet I felt on edge as we continued the climb. *Why did we decide to go this way?* I thought.

About halfway up the boulder field, my friend climbing in front of me lost her balance and fell backward on top of me. The impact sent me flying backward as well. I landed on a nearby boulder. Thankfully, we were both fine physically. However, I immediately started crying. "Why are we doing this?" I cried. "I don't want to hike anymore. I just want to go home!" Mom graciously comforted me, assuring me that everything was going to be okay. "We can come back another time to finish the trail," she soothed. I was so mentally shaken from the fall that I gave up my resolve and didn't summit the mountain that day. Mom and I hiked back to the car by ourselves. We waited for the rest of our group in the parking lot. Thankfully, Mom didn't demean my fearfulness but rather offered grace and understanding.

Mom, Laurel, and I conquered the Cathedral Trail several years later. During that same trip, we also completed the perilous Knife Edge Trail. The entire hike was incredibly difficult. Mom encouraged us the entire way. We finished enthusiastically, excited for our accomplishment. Laurel and I successfully hiked Mt. Katahdin frequently throughout high school. We invited friends to join us and completed many rewarding summits to both Pamola Peak and Baxter Peak. Clear summer days above Mt. Katahdin's tree line are exhilarating. The views are breathtaking, and the adrenaline rush is addictive. Our Baxter State Park adventures fostered a love for the mountains. My siblings and I still enjoy hiking today.

In Millinocket, the warmth of summer changes rapidly to fall. Cool breezes begin to blow, bringing with them a feeling of brisk excitement. As a kid, fall was my most favorite time of year. It still is! I love it for many reasons: my birthday is in October, cross-country running is in full force, jeans and sweaters come out of the closet, and my two favorite foods — soup and hot tea — are back in season. The magnificent transformation of the forests adds exhilaration to my enjoyment. Maine's dense, green foliage transforms into a fiery landscape. Multiple variations of yellow, orange, and red explode throughout the horizon. The colors are breathtaking. I find it difficult to describe the magnificence of a Maine fall. It is truly a little piece of heaven on earth. My family knew fall by another name as well. It was called "Hunting Season." When he wasn't guiding fall hunts, Dad often hunted alone. But one year, the whole family participated in an exciting moose hunt.

The moose population was prolific during our years in Maine. Even today, Maine contains more moose than any other state in the lower 48. Despite this, the annual moose hunt was available by permit only, and only 4,080 permits were issued each year. They were given out through a points and lottery system. Having a large family worked in Dad's favor. He submitted each qualifying family member's name every year in hopes of earning enough points to get selected.

In 1996, Dad's name was drawn! Dad is typically mild-mannered and not given to emotional extremes. Yet he nearly burst with excitement as he informed the family that we were going to harvest a moose together! I was nearly 14, and Seth was only 6. Dad carefully prepared each of us for the hunt. He gently coached my sisters, brother, and me on proper gun handling and sportsmanship. We frequented the local sand pits and practiced shooting a variety of rifles. Even though I didn't ever personally harvest an animal, I enjoyed that time with my dad. To this day I appreciate Dad's care as he taught me appropriate sportsmanship.

Maine forests are incredibly dense with old and new trees. The thick underbrush can make walking through the woods nearly impossible at times. Hunters often scout moose by driving the logging roads. This prevents some of the challenges that come when tracking these lanky animals. Our family used this technique. We squished into my father's truck and slowly drove the remote, dirt roads.

The day of our hunt was perfect. The October air was crisp yet warm as the sunshine peeked through the scattered clouds. The trees were already past their prime, and some of the brightly colored leaves blanketed the ground. Their aromatic fragrance filled the air as if declaring their readiness for the upcoming winter months. Most of Maine's songbirds had already flown south. However, the remaining birds chirped happily, singing songs of pure joy.

Dad once again dressed in his woodsman finery: warm wool pants, knee-high rubber boots, cozy flannel shirt, green wool hat, and, of course, his bright orange wool hunting vest. Dad made sure we all wore distinctive hunter's orange.

Dad's blue eyes are as sharp as that of an eagle. He's most attentive when he's hunting. Dad drove slowly that day. He methodically weaved the truck back and forth along the road as he searched for signs of the majestic animals. Dad found a clearing, pulled off the road, and announced his plan. "Everyone get out!" he said, "I am going to call in a moose!"

We all piled out of the truck and settled into a hiding spot behind a large granite boulder. Although silent, the forest felt alive with anticipation. Dad positioned himself in front of us all and hid behind a cluster of saplings. His gun that day was his muzzle loader. It is a powerful rifle. It also has only one shot at a time. That adds an additional challenge should the hunter need a second or third shot.

Dad's moose calls are forever embedded in my memory. He didn't use any modern contraptions. He used his voice, perfectly mimicking the high-pitched bellow of a cow in the rut. I don't remember how long we sat there, huddled behind the rock. Yet all of a sudden, a bull's bellow echoed through the forest. Dad and the bull interacted back and forth, speaking their own language of love.

Soon we heard the bull thrashing through the brush, aggressively seeking his female pursuit. All too quickly, the bull stood in the clearing, desperately searching for the caller. Dad remained hidden behind the saplings and took his first shot. Even though his aim was successful, the shot didn't even phase the moose. He turned his majestic head and glanced at Dad, as if mocking his attempt. Dad hastily reloaded his gun. He inserted the black powder and spherical lead ball, using his ramrod to secure all appropriate measures. As the smoke from the second shot wafted around my father, the moose was startled and began running away. Dad quickly reloaded a third time and administered the final shot. We were jubilant and joyfully celebrated Dad's success.

The moose fell within one hundred yards of the truck. It took the rest of the day to harvest the animal. Bull moose can weigh up to 1,500 pounds, and ours was well over 1,000 pounds. We ended the moose hunt with a prayer of thanksgiving. We were grateful for the successful hunt and also thankful for the meat we'd enjoy for the remainder of the year. Stews, roasts, and burgers were abundant. To this day moose meat is one of my favorite wild game meats.

As I think back on these outdoor adventures, I feel overwhelmed with gratitude. I am thankful my parents cultivated time outside. Like the verse at the beginning of the chapter says, the heavens and earth declare the majesty of their Creator. That verse's message is similar to a quote by George Washington Carver. He says, "I love to think of nature as an unlimited broadcasting station, through which God speaks to us every hour, if we will just tune in." I know I definitely feel closer to God when I'm outside! To this day,

I love the fresh air. When the sun shines on my face, I feel energized and full of life!

What about you? What do you enjoy about the outdoors? Is it the sunshine? Do you enjoy hiking through the woods and listening to the birds? What about watching the clouds? Or experiencing the ocean's waves as they crash upon the shore? Or standing on top of a mountain and enjoying a view? Aren't the outdoors truly magnificent? And what about the seasons? What unique seasonal experiences did you have? My childhood included smelting in the spring, hiking mountains in the summer, and moose hunting in the fall. But what about you? I am sure you have some really special memories, too.

As an adult, I now seek out unique seasonal experiences for my kids. Currently, one of our family's favorite summertime activities is backpacking. In Colorado, mountains and trails are abundant, and opportunities for wilderness excursions are easily accessible. My kids thoroughly enjoy our backpacking adventures. By default, our trips instill many important life skills. My kids learn how to maintain a good attitude when fatigued. They discover the value of packing out their trash and outdoor safety. We enjoy building memories as a family. And we all rediscover peace and beauty as we step away from technology. I've found technology can squelch creativity. While it is convenient, it oftentimes adds to the frenetic pace of modern-day life and steals joy and contentment. Have you found that to be true as well?

I've given an example of my family's favorite summertime activity. However, outdoor time can be simple and may be right outside your doorstep. My home is close to a nature preserve. In Colorado Springs, we call these areas "Open Spaces." Recreational trails wind through most open spaces, providing people with opportunities to enjoy nature. My neighborhood's open space is a hidden gem within the busyness of the city. Miles of walking trails, magnificent mountain views, and a spring fed pond make the area special. Dozens of red-winged black birds make their homes in the reeds surrounding the pond. Mule deer, ducks, owls, and bobcats wander through the acreage. This area is across the street from my home, and I enjoy it every day. Our family makes memories here, too.

At the open space's pond, my kids discovered fishing. Throughout the summer months, they frequent the pond for hours each day. They catch and release the sunnies and smallmouth bass that swim in the depths. They also build forts within the scrub oak and cultivate adventures around the stream. As a family, we walk through the trails. Most days, I run the trails by myself and experience the purple and pink sunrises that streak through the morning sky. The open space provides a simple place for enjoying God's creation and rediscovering peace for each day.

What seasonal memories do you treasure from your childhood? Which aspects make these recollections so special to you? Whether you are single or have a family, could seasonal rhythms and natural beauty help you cultivate wonder and peace? And rediscover joy again? As I recalled the outdoor adventures of my childhood, I was reminded of the peace and joy that come whenever I step outside. I think I will remain mindful of this moving forward. I will step into the sun and fresh air when I feel anxious. Practice slowing down enough to listen to the birds. Stop to admire the beauty around me. I think doing these things will produce gratitude and wonder.

Would you consider the magnificent Creator as you reflect on the beauty around you? Your adventures don't have to be extravagant; they can be simple. As you step into the outdoors, I pray you will feel refreshed and revived in every way.

Rediscovering
BEAUTY IN SEASONS

To everything there is a season,
A time for every purpose under heaven...
He has made everything beautiful for its own time.

— Ecclesiastes 3:1, 11 (NKJV)

God, grant me the serenity
To accept the things I cannot change,
The courage to change the things I can,
And the wisdom to know the difference.

— The Serenity Prayer

CHAPTER NINE

Winter comes early in Millinocket, and it camps out for months. The deciduous trees drop their final leaves by the end of October. Cool winds drive away the colors as well as all remnants of warmth. Snow starts to fall by the end of November. The white blanket generously wraps itself around the land and doesn't roll back until April. Every bird flies south. Animals go into hiding. Fish swim far below the frozen surface. Temperatures routinely hover below freezing. In some months, temperatures frequently plummet well below zero degrees Fahrenheit — and stay there.

My parents were familiar with New England winters. Dad grew up in the Catskills of New York, and Mom is from Massachusetts. Even so, they were not prepared for the prolonged winters of Maine. It penetrates everything.

Our first Maine winter shocked Mom and Dad. Roads covered with layer upon layer of snow. Lakes froze so thick that by the time January rolled around, fleets of ice fishermen fearlessly drove their trucks across the ice. Snowbanks piled high on each street. They almost reached the power line wires before commercial-sized snow blowers and dump trucks removed the towering mounds. This extra snow was dumped into local rivers. Once the rivers froze over, trucks transported snow to the outskirts of town. It piled high, creating winter mountains. These icy mounds didn't melt until May. As a child, I witnessed both grit and resolve from the town's residents. These traits were admirable — and necessary — if you were going to withstand the long, frigid winters.

There were many interesting practices that Mainers implemented to cope with the sub-zero temperatures and heavy snowfall. When temperatures stayed below zero, homeowners who didn't have a garage (like us), charged their vehicles overnight to ensure they would start in the morning and run all day. Oversized extension cords wound stiffly from driveways into houses.

Measures were also taken with older homes. Our home didn't have storm windows, so preserving heat became a challenge. Mom and Dad quickly discovered the practice of stapling heavy-duty plastic over each window's trim to add an extra dimension of protection. Our clear window panes remained cloudy all winter long. However, the limited light was better than abundant drafts! Since we got so much snow, everyone owned a snow blower and shovel to keep the sidewalks and driveways cleared. We also used

long-handled snow rakes to pull heavy snow from roofs
to prevent cave-ins. Despite the cold and snow, my family
embraced the winter with open arms. Some of my fondest
memories are from the winters.

Through local friends, Mom discovered the sport
of cross-country skiing. She then introduced it to us.
Throughout my growing-up years, Millinocket maintained
two cross-country ski areas. Our family's personal favorite
was called the Bait Hole. The Bait Hole is located on
Brownville Road, only 3 miles south of our Knox Street
home. This sanctuary offered six miles of cross-country ski
and snowshoe trails winding through peaceful forests. The
trails provide scenic views of Mt. Katahdin and Elbow Lake.

Always one to enjoy the outdoors, Mom encouraged
each one of us kids to ski. In my early days of learning,
I often ended up in a heap in the snow. I was not a
particularly coordinated child and frequently tangled my
skis and poles. I remember stumbling along after Mom
as a young nine-year-old, desperately trying to keep up. I
wanted to master whatever I was doing immediately, so I
quickened my pace in hopes of proficiency. My attempts
failed miserably over and over again! I often succumbed
to tears, complaining I could not do this sport. Mom was
incredibly patient. She encouraged me to keep going — just
until I stopped complaining — and then we would return
home. My sister, Laurel, was much more patient than I was.
Because of her less hurried pace, she mastered the methodi-
cal rhythm of classical skiing quicker than I did. When they
grew older, my other siblings joined us as well.

Year after year, Mom took us to the Bait Hole. Each year we improved. The day came when we all enjoyed the sport just as much, or even more, than Mom did! From that point on, Mom always had someone who eagerly joined her for an afternoon ski. Our ski adventures at the Bait Hole were so much fun! I didn't even attempt downhill skiing until high school. To this day, we all enjoy both cross-country and downhill skiing. However, of the two, most of us prefer cross-country skiing.

Throughout our high school years, Laurel and I competed with the Stearns High School cross-country ski team. It remained one of the school's varsity sports until we graduated in 2000. Our team was a small, eclectic mix of students. We had so much fun conditioning and competing. The team practiced and raced both classic and skate skiing.

Before snow adequately covered the local trails, we practiced indoors. We completed drills in the gym. We ran halls and stairs throughout the high school. Once there was enough snow, we transitioned to the track. By December, the forested trails were ready. Practice started immediately after school, and we skied as far as we could go before the sunset. Practice always seemed short due to the limited light.

I developed grit during the frigid practices and races. I distinctly remember my senior year. Throughout that winter, daytime temperatures remained consistently below zero. However, practices and meets were rarely canceled. That year my body was usually numb with cold by the time I finished skiing. Even so, I only have fond memories of the sport.

Racing was really fun! Cross-country ski racing is very individualized. Competitors start 10 seconds apart. Racers compete alone, passing competitors one by one. It's common to be alone for miles. Skiers have to stay mentally tough and focused to perform well. The sub-zero days can be especially challenging.

Initially, Laurel and I didn't perform very well. I finished at the back of the pack my freshman year, taking over thirty minutes to complete the 5k race. But I loved every minute of the competition. With much practice, as well as gentle guidance from our talented teammate, Julie, both Laurel and I improved tremendously. By the time we reached our senior year, Laurel and I led our team at the state competition, cutting our 5k time in half from when we started four years earlier.

I remember mentally coaching myself to go as fast as I could. It was a mind trick to persevere so I could get back to the warmth of the bus. My face was always the first part of my body to freeze, followed by my hands and then my feet. I remember feeling like a human ice cube by the time I finished. I was always so excited to get back to the bus where I could unthaw. Aside from the large state meets, most of our ski meets occurred in remotely forested locations. Our school bus served as the team's locker room. We defrosted on the bus and exchanged stories of our races. There was a beautiful camaraderie among all of us. We celebrated our challenges and victories together. And we all developed incredible grit. I only recall one race being canceled due to weather. On that particular day, the daytime temperature was -20F, and the windchill drove the temperature even lower. Even so, I remember feeling disappointed about the cancellation. I would have still raced had I been given the opportunity.

Our school also generally remained open. Cancellations due to weather were rare. I only recall one year when we enjoyed consecutively canceled school days. This happened during the New England ice storm of 1998. Millinocket was not hit as hard as Upstate New York and other parts of central Maine. I still remember that storm. Spherical ice granules covered the ground day after day for five days straight. The ground accumulated inch upon inch of ice. Ironically, school remained open for the first several days of the storm. It wasn't until Maine was declared a national disaster area that Millinocket canceled school for the rest of the week.

During that storm, thousands of limbs and power lines snapped under the weight of the ice. Hundreds of thousands of Mainers lost their power. Thankfully, many people, like us, had more than one heat source. We relied on our wood stove when our power went out. Despite the devastation, the winter wonderland was magnificent. Ice surrounded everything. Trees gleamed like diamonds. Every last twig and pine needle sparkled and shone. It was beautiful.

One of the other ways to play outside in the winter was ice skating. The Millinocket Park and Recreation Department supported an outdoor skating rink. Once daytime temperatures stayed below freezing, the Rec Department flooded a large field next to the high school. The rink sported a rustic warming hut. It provided a simple space to lace up skates, rest, and defrost. Lights conveniently surrounded the field. As previously mentioned, daylight was minimal during December and January. My siblings and I spent many late afternoons and evenings skating under the lights.

During our years in Millinocket, the community was stable and safe. Many kids were given the freedom to independently enjoy the town's activities. Once we turned twelve, Laurel and I frequently cared for our younger siblings. Many winter afternoons involved skating or sledding. Because we couldn't yet drive, we used our sleds for transportation. We trekked downhill for one mile to the skating rink. We usually skated for an hour or more. Sometimes we alternated skating with sledding. A large hill loomed close to the ice rink. It was affectionately called the Ski Tow, as it had accommodated downhill skiers in its earlier years. We enjoyed the afternoon fun until we were either too tired or too cold. Then we made the one-mile, uphill trudge back home. We always arrived rosy-cheeked and hungry, often just in time for dinner.

Another great winter memory involves snowmobiling. Due to the large amounts of snow in Millinocket, sidewalks convert into snowmobile trails throughout the winter. Residents and out-of-town tourists have access to hundreds of miles of trails. While I'm sure my perception wasn't totally accurate, it seemed as though everyone in Millinocket owned at least one, if not two, snowmobiles. During our later years in town, our family purchased an old snowmobile. It wasn't fancy, but it was so much fun to ride!

We all learned to drive it. Mom and Dad allowed us to use it independently. We enjoyed this freedom and used the snowmobile regularly. Because we lived only two blocks from the edge of town, we had easy access to snowmobile trails. Mom and Dad frequently reminded us of trail etiquette and safety. The most important rule was to stay on the trail at all times. You must never, ever, venture off the trail. Your heavy snowmobile could easily sink into the depths of snow and be lost until spring.

While I never experienced any snowmobiling challenges, Helene and Seth had quite an adventure. The following story is shared by my sister, Helene.

One bright and cold sunny afternoon, Seth and I had the brilliant idea of going for a drive together — destination unknown. We knew we had to drive slowly on the snow-packed roads until we got out of town. Once onto the trails, we could amp it up. I drove, and Seth sat behind me. His arms rotated between hugging my waist and holding the bar behind the cushioned seat. We quickly arrived at the trail and excitedly increased our speed. We zipped through the clearings. The mixture of cold air and muffled breath from our helmets blended. The trails were empty — it was just the two of us enjoying our "new" 1987, yellow snowmobile.

The sun visits northern Maine for very limited hours during the winter months. When we noticed the sun creeping toward the horizon, we turned around. The trail ride back to town paralleled our trip out. Although a different trail, we were familiar with our route home. A couple of miles from home, a large pine tree blocked the trail. Spiky branches and palms of pine spread all over the place. I was only eleven years old and thought there was absolutely no way over the fallen tree. I turned the handlebars right, venturing into the snowy woods. Seth's voice yelled to me from behind. "The snowmobile can easily cross the fallen tree," he said. Being the big sister, I overrode his warning. "There's no possible way," I reasoned. I slowly drove off the trail and into the woods.

Within moments, I quickly faced the consequences of my poor decision. The big machine suddenly dropped beneath the sparkling, white surface. Three feet of fluffy snow immediately enveloped us. I stood up quickly. I was almost 5'10", and yet I was up to my thighs in snow. The snow covered Seth to his waist. We sat, stunned for a moment. Then Seth's voice piped up from behind me. "I think we're stuck," he said.

I started revving the engine, trying to proceed. We only sank deeper into the mound of snow and did not make any progress. Seth began to panic. He experienced many outings with Dad. These gave him much more knowledge of the situation, though I didn't dare admit it to him. We quickly went into problem-solving mode. We took turns between revving the engine and pushing from behind.

After multiple failed attempts, we both started panicking. Dusk set in. The temperature quickly sunk below zero. Seth started to cry. I inwardly started to spiral. Thoughts raced through my head. What if we get stuck in the woods? Should we abandon the snowmobile? Can we hike back to the trail and make our way home on foot?

I knew that Route 11, Quakish Lake — and home — were still several miles away. With what little daylight we had left, neither outcome seemed promising. So I just sat and started praying, "Please God, please God, please God."

I don't remember if it was my idea or Seth's (probably Seth's), but we decided to sit on the very back of the snowmobile.

We adjusted our weight to give the rear suspension some traction. As we revved the engine, we gained several inches of ground. We did it again, and we gained a few more inches. We continued that process until we miraculously dug our way out of the deep cold snow. We made the ride home in silence. Thoughts swirled through our heads. We breathed sighs of relief and barely heard the noise from the engine. Even after we arrived home, our bodies still shook from panic.

Now as adults, Seth and I laugh in disbelief at the entire situation. I am still amazed we were able to adventure into the middle of "nowhere" at our age (nowhere — which is essentially everywhere when you're beyond a town's limits in northern Maine). I am thankful God's hand protected us. I truly believe that God heard my cries and helped us navigate back to safety. The snowmobile adventure was a bonding experience for me and Seth — once he started talking to me again.

Another comical winter memory occurred during a blizzard. Laurel and I were about sixteen years old at the time. We frequently enjoyed the freedom of maneuvering about in our old-fashioned pickup truck. That particular afternoon, we connected with a friend in Bangor, the small city previously mentioned which is located 70 miles south of Millinocket. During our visit, snowflakes started falling and accumulated rapidly. However, we prolonged our visit as long as possible. We eventually wrapped up our time when we recognized the worsening conditions.

Snow removal in Maine is of the highest priority. Roads are meticulously cared for and cleared. Yet, on this particular evening, the falling snow accumulated quite quickly. The highway was an uninterrupted pathway of white. At least eight inches of snow covered the road. Our truck was one of the few vehicles out that night. We rapidly blazed our trail northward. Our speed sent snow billowing amidst both sides of our truck.

Now you must understand that driving in ice and snow is a skill that all New England adolescents learn. If we didn't, activities would be on hold for months at a time. Driving in the storm that evening was a somewhat ordinary occurrence. Even so, Dad always encouraged Laurel and me to be mindful of the weather and eliminate any need for speed during the winter months. Most of the time we heeded his advice. On this particular evening, we did not.

Empty roads and highways are common in Maine. There were even fewer vehicles out that evening. I only recall passing one truck during the 70-mile trip home. We took full advantage of the emptiness. While we kept our truck below the speed limit, we drove faster than we should have — and enjoyed every minute of it! Our headlights illuminated the beautiful landscape. We blared our radio and nonchalantly sang songs during our drive. We arrived home in record time and walked into our cozy kitchen with elevated spirits.

Shortly thereafter, the kitchen door opened. This time Dad walked through. His face was grim and a serious demeanor enveloped his normally jovial being. He addressed Laurel and me with gravity. "I was passed by a truck on the highway," he began. "The truck was going much too fast for an evening such as this..." his voice trailed off as he allowed his words to sink in.

My heart immediately dropped to my toes. I felt sick as I realized the only vehicle Laurel and I had passed on the highway that night had been my father.

Dad wasn't one to elevate his voice when making a point. He had a way of communicating through his countenance. I will never forget his demeanor that evening. I felt the weight of his concern and caution. I've always been one who desired to please and never disappoint. I hadn't meant to be careless or immature. As he looked at me, I intuitively grasped how my actions could have negatively impacted my sister and me, or even worse, someone else. From that point on, I determined to become more aware of my surroundings and the impact my decisions could have on those around me.

I recently drove my parents through snowy conditions in Colorado. Dad quietly observed my driving from his position in the passenger seat. He gently admonished me to slow down once more. This time, I heeded his advice. We laughed together as we recalled my highway adventure from twenty-five years before.

As I wrap up this chapter, you might be wondering, "What could winter possibly teach me?" I've been contemplating that too!

I believe there can be lessons in every moment and every season — both literal and figurative. In the literal sense, winters in Maine are tough. It seems as though they will never end. Darkness descends and light is limited. The snow is deep and the conditions are harsh. Life during winter is more challenging than life in the summer. But it also has a quiet beauty. I think of freshly fallen snow, pure white and peaceful. I think of the landscape, resting for months as if tucked into bed. I think of the people, gritty and strong, doing what needs to be done to make it through. And I think of my family, exploring new activities in the midst of the cold.

Life is sometimes like this too. Tough. Deep. Challenging. Yet at the same time, quietly beautiful. Full of rest. It can require us to do what needs to be done to make it through. Sometimes it surprises us with new people or activities to enjoy in the midst of it.

What season do you find yourself in? Spring? Summer? Fall? Winter? It's been a winter season for me. If you are like me, I pray you will build grit, cultivate rest, and discover beauty. God gently reminds me of a truth about each season — it never lasts forever. And I am also reminded of the Scripture at the beginning of this chapter: "To everything there is a season, a time for every purpose under heaven...God has made everything beautiful for its own time." Ecclesiastes 3:1, 11 (NLT). Let's embrace the season we're in! And in time, it will all be made beautiful.

Rediscovering
IDENTITY

———————— 66 ————————

I am sure of this, that He who began
a good work in you will bring it to
completion at the day of Jesus Christ.

— Philippians 1:6 (ESV)

———————— 66 ————————

Fear is not my future, You are, You are!

Sickness is not my story, You are, You are!

Heartbreak is not my home, You are, You are!

Death is not the end, You are, You are!

— Maverick City Music*

CHAPTER TEN

Over the past twenty years, I've jumped into personal development. I'm fascinated by the vast differences and similarities of people. For those of you who are familiar with the Enneagram, I am a 3 with a 2 wing. I lean toward "Performance" and "Helping" (after reading through this book, I am sure there are no surprises there!) Efficiency and achievement drive me, while sensing and meeting the needs of others motivates me. In addition to my study of the Enneagram, I've learned about Myers-Briggs personality types. I am an INFJ — introverted, yet a lover of people, highly intuitive — though more internally aware of others' needs than my own — deeply emotional, idealistic, frank (sometimes to a fault), determined, complex, and fiercely loyal. Basically, I advocate to right the wrongs I see in this world.

Every personality has strengths. They also have areas of weakness. Growth occurs when you are aware of your strengths and weaknesses. INFJs are the rarest of all personality types. Maybe that explains why I often feel misunderstood, insecure in my own skin, and driven to prove my value. Over and over again, I lose myself in my pursuits. Horses, running, friendships, work — I easily become enmeshed in whatever I do.

Many benefits come from passionately materializing my ideals. Yet when I earn my value from my accomplishments or relationships, I find myself in trouble. Again, and again. I truly struggle to "just be." Internally, my obsessive tendencies produce high anxiety. I have to work hard to rest and to remain at peace (that sounds like an oxymoron, doesn't it?). Can you relate at all to what I am saying?

Living as a creative, purpose-driven, highly relational-emotional, future-focused individual can be extremely exhausting! I often covet the lives of people who live life contented and fully engaged in the present. My incredible husband is one of these people.

Through writing this book, God reminded me of the values that define my life: community, serving, compassion, resourcefulness, imagination, entrepreneurship, adventure, faith, and family. These values give my life purpose and direction. God also gently challenged me to hold these values loosely. Many times He asked me to feel His delight. He embraced me with His grace, peace, and love. And not because of anything I was doing or anyone I was helping, but *just because I am His precious child.*

As I thought through different ways to wrap up this book, my husband challenged me to share about my broken years. Years that I sometimes wish I could erase. I wasn't sure that I wanted to write about this piece of my story. It is a very painful part of my past. The details lurk hidden and unwanted in the back of my mind. *Would this chapter of my story offer any value?* I wondered. As I contemplated this, I decided my previous challenges may propagate hope — because my dark burdens have since become a beautiful rainbow of promise. They illuminate God's destiny of healing and wholeness for those who pursue Him.

It's with great vulnerability and humility that I share this piece of my story. Yet I pray my authenticity cultivates humble relatability. As I dive into this chapter, I hope it encourages you. And if you or a loved one is struggling with addiction, long-term illness, or seemingly insurmountable challenges, I pray you will find rest in the One whose unconditional love is more expansive than ever imagined.

To begin, allow me to share pieces of my rich heritage, starting with the Reed family. They passed down a legacy of food from generation to generation. My great-grandmother, Helene Lunning, unexpectedly became a single mother to her three young children during World War II. Her husband was abruptly killed on the SS Dorchester when a German U-boat torpedoed his ship. Most of the ship's passengers died that day. When Helene received the news of her husband's death, she knew she would have to make some changes to provide for her young family. She didn't know she was expecting a baby. Helene had her only son nine months later.

After the death of her husband, Helene moved her family from New York City to Upstate New York. There she used her cooking skills and helped her mother operate a boarding house. Her parents were immigrants from Czechoslovakia and worked hard on their family farm. Three years later, when her mother passed away, Helene purchased her own property. Initially the home had no running water, electricity, or other modern amenities. Determined to provide for her family, Helene took in summer boarders and housed hunters in the fall. Helene specialized in creating rich dishes of homemade egg noodles, creamy sauces, and savory soups. She passed the heritage of food to my dad's mom, Suzanne Lunning Reed Stetka. We grandkids affectionately call her Nana.

Nana is an incredible cook. As a child, I loved going to my Nana and Pop-pop Reed's. Their modest home sits in Mongaup Valley, a rustic community in the foothills of the Catskills. Although remote, their home always overflowed with people. Nana and Pop-pop welcomed everyone, and food was the common ingredient that bound them all together. Anyone who stepped into Nana's kitchen left full in their stomach and heart.

My father carried on the culinary tradition by pursuing his degree as a premier chef and baker. He started cooking consistently throughout his teens and cultivated his skills as a pastry chef. Although he left the industry during our Maine years, Dad routinely initiated camaraderie and connection around the kitchen table. It was in this environment that my siblings and I were raised.

From a young age, Laurel and I embraced responsibilities around the kitchen. I always enjoyed the creativity of cooking. By the time we were 12 years old, Laurel and I comfortably used our commercial-sized gas stove and oven. We shouldered the weekly responsibilities of baking chocolate chip cookies and bread. We preserved jam and baked pies with Mom. Our daily menu was simple. We rotated through stew, spaghetti, venison, and fish. We also enjoyed lots of vegetables and potatoes from our garden. Despite the simplicity, the food always satisfied our stomachs.

More important than the menu was the atmosphere I felt around the table. As I mentioned before, our door was always open. It seems fitting that people walked through the front porch of our home directly into our cozy kitchen. Everyone entered with ease and made themselves at home around the table. Food was a tool for connection. Mom and Dad liberally served coffee, tea, and cookies. While sitting at the table, they offered their listening ear, laughter, and love. I also experienced these things around the table.

One of my favorite times of year was December. Mom set aside our school routine for the entire month! Together we prepared our hearts and our home for the Christmas season. Food was a big part of that preparation. Because Mom and Helene have Type I Diabetes, treats were not normally part of our everyday lives. Mom remained intentional with our family's diet to make sure she and Helene stayed on track with their blood sugars. However, everything changed when Mom pulled out her holiday recipes! In December the kitchen became a flurry of flour, sugar, and butter.

We shaped and decorated traditional sugar cookies. Crunchy birds' nests cookies, rolled in walnuts and filled with homemade strawberry preserves, offered bite-sized goodness. We melted and stirred fluffy marshmallow cream, chocolate chips, and butter into creamy fudge. And my personal favorites were peanut butter blossoms, complete with Hershey's kisses gently pressed into the center. After we finished the treats, we distributed the culinary goodness among neighbors and friends. My heart overflowed with joy as we shared these goodies.

In addition to baking Christmas cookies, December held the anticipation of a Christmas party! While both of my parents are introverts and prefer ample time to themselves, they also value community. So, every couple of years they hosted a Christmas party at our home. We invited everyone we knew! Dad set aside his taxidermy work and returned to his culinary roots. He created delicious dishes such as stuffed mushrooms, homemade meatballs, and savory dipping sauces.

I'm still amazed at the amount of people who packed into our modest home. People crammed into the kitchen and living room. Often, more people were standing than sitting as our seating options were quite limited. Since we didn't have a coat closet anywhere in the house, my parents' bedroom became a mound of coats and jackets. One of my jobs at the party was running to and from the bedroom to dispose of guests' jackets then later rummaging through the pile to retrieve them. I remember feeling full of contentment and peace, welcoming and visiting with everyone who came through the doors. The commonality of food was imprinted in my mind as a positive way to connect with others.

While food was a tradition on Dad's side of the family, Mom's side valued outdoor activities. Grandpa James Graham was an Irish immigrant. My fondest memories with Grandma and Grandpa Graham involve walking amidst their orchard. They maintained a beautiful property in central Massachusetts. Flower gardens, vegetable gardens, and fruit trees produced abundant harvests every year. Their property provided ample space to walk and play. Whenever we visited Grandpa and Grandma, we walked outdoors in the fresh air. A storyteller to his core, Grandpa jovially relayed tales of his youthful expeditions to us grandkids. He shared stories of his adventures, including running cross-country throughout the hills of Ireland.

Throughout my growing up years, Mom didn't frequent a gym. Yet she stayed active and fit. Mom encouraged us to get outside every day, and she often initiated outdoor activities. I had other great examples as well. Mom's sister, my Aunt Cindy, adopted my grandfather's sport. She was an avid runner and annually competed in the prestigious Boston Marathon. Laurel and I admired our aunt's determination and dedication. We listened to her running stories each year. It was my Aunt Cindy's example that inspired me to try running in high school.

I've always loved being active. As I mentioned before, Mom introduced me to hiking and cross-country skiing when I was little, and I really enjoyed those activities. Laurel and I also rode our bikes and rollerbladed continuously throughout the summer months. We annually participated in the Millinocket Summer Rec Department's programs of gymnastics and swimming. I even ran Hershey Track and Field one summer and made it to the state competition. However, it wasn't until the end of my sophomore year of high school when I truly discovered my love for running.

As a high school freshman and sophomore, I thoroughly enjoyed the cross-country ski team. Because of my positive experience, I decided to run track. I walked on the team not knowing much. I did not have natural speed, but I found I had endurance. I discovered I could keep running when others grew tired, so I ran the 800m and 1600m events. To my surprise, I found out I had some talent in the sport. Since Laurel and I did everything together, she joined the track team as well. Our first year she competed in shorter sprints and hurdle races. It wasn't until she transitioned to the longer distances the following year that she started enjoying the sport as well.

Track was so much fun! I loved pushing my body during practice and competitions, and being part of a team was fulfilling! To this day, joining the track team remains one of the defining moments of my life. Distance running provided me with so many blessings following my Maine years.

I also ran on the cross-country team. Our team was small. Those who are familiar with the sport know a complete team needs only five runners. Despite this minuscule number, our school didn't have a full men's team, and on some occasions, even our women's team was incomplete. Even so, I fell in love with the sport. I felt incredible joy when I ran.

Laurel and I shocked ourselves when we placed second and third in our first cross-country race. The course wove through the forests of Dover Foxcroft. I felt so nervous at that first race — I had no idea where I would place or how I would run. My parents weren't there to watch, and my coach didn't know what to expect either. Imagine my surprise as I settled into the front pack rather quickly and finished within seconds of first place. Laurel finished right behind me.

Laurel and I felt privileged to compete in the Maine State Meet that year for both cross country and track. During our junior year of high school, our 4 x 800m relay team placed second in the entire state. Our relay team won nearly every meet that season and desired to qualify for the New England competition. Due to an unfortunate misunderstanding of the rules, our team was disqualified at the state meet (one of our teammates "cheered too close to the track"). Otherwise, we would have met our season goal and progressed to the New England competition.

I experienced many achievements with running. Yet I had challenges as well. During cross country, I struggled profusely with activity-induced asthma. I never had breathing issues before. Yet when I raced longer distances, my airways constricted and my body shut down. Despite medical evaluations and inhalers, I found little relief. Additionally, unwanted tension mounted between Laurel and me. We'd always been competitive, but we pushed each other constructively. As we experienced running success, people started comparing us in ways that felt uncomfortable and stressful. I loved running, and I loved my sister. I wasn't sure how to navigate these challenges.

Up until that point, beauty blossomed from both parts of my heritage. I enjoyed sports, and I enjoyed food. Because of my activity level, I could eat whatever I wanted without any thought of the results. After I started running, I became more aware of food's impact on my body's appearance and performance.

My petite build suits endurance sports, and I'm naturally toned. I never thought much about my appearance though. Once I started running, I routinely received interesting, sometimes sarcastic, comments from peers about my body. Laurel did too. I am sure the comments were meant in jest. Although I portrayed a determined and strong image externally, internally I felt self-conscious. I desired to excel in every area of my life. This desire for perfection and control began to drive me in an unhealthy direction. As with many enjoyments in life, lines between healthy habits and problematic patterns can sometimes become blurred. This happened to me.

Mom never dieted or talked about her weight. Yet Mom's friends confided in her because she was so healthy. She offered a listening ear and encouraged her friends in their journeys. I still remember exactly where I was standing when I overheard Mom's friend discussing her diet. They sat at the kitchen table. I stood quietly in the doorway between the kitchen and the living room. At that age, I preferred to listen instead of being in the spotlight. I remained unnoticed — they didn't even realize I was there. Mom's friend shared her realization that dieting wasn't necessary if you only ate until you were full. She was so excited about the new habits she'd implemented.

As I listened, seeds of curiosity were planted in my mind. *What a novel idea*, I thought. *Can I become so in tune with my body, eating only when I am hungry... and only until I am slightly full? Maybe this will help my performance as a runner!* I intuitively implemented a new mindset around food. Over the next year, I began a slow decline. I developed an obsessive-compulsive disorder revolving around running and eating. I regretfully share that my actions negatively impacted Laurel as well. She frequently followed my lead. This area was no different — Laurel modeled my destructive behavior.

Food had been one of the greatest joys in our home. Now it was a point of dissension and conflict. My parents helplessly watched my sister and me neglect the needs of our active bodies. Meal times were no longer peaceful or full of connection but explosive and fractured. The relationship between my parents and me became strained. It got so bad that Laurel and I even explored alternative living situations at that time, though we didn't follow through with it.

Many adults approached my parents with concern for my sister and me. However, very few peers knew of our struggles. From my senior year forward, I lost myself in the sport of running. It was one of the only areas where I felt alive and in control. At the same time, my thoughts and habits spiraled lower and lower. I began to despise myself. As with all addictions and disorders, you often don't even comprehend you have a problem until it's too late. Such was the case with me. What started as an innocent exploration turned into an all-consuming obsession and ended up dominating my life for the next fifteen years.

During these years of my life, I neglected the values I learned as a child. I moved away from serving others to serving myself. Most of my thoughts were self-centered and self-focused. My friendship with Laurel fractured as we competed against one another in unhealthy ways.

I progressed to become a gifted collegiate runner. I earned MVP multiple times and won two national titles. Yet my unhealthy fixations caused tension between me and the women on my team. I couldn't fully enjoy many female friendships. Several years into my college career, I plummeted with the consequences of my condition.

Sometimes it takes hitting rock bottom before you can move forward. My rock-bottom moment came when I was nineteen, during my junior year of college. Up until that point, I performed at the top of the women's team throughout all three sports: cross country, indoor track, and outdoor track. My college classes were challenging but manageable. I expected my trajectory to continue. However, my body, mind, and spirit had suffered just a little too long. In the fall of my junior year, everything began to unravel.

First of all, my pre-med courses proved more rigorous and demanding than I'd anticipated. Learning has always come naturally to me. But that year, Organic Chemistry and Physics challenged my comprehension. I spent hours seeking help from professors and peers. Feelings of inadequacy constantly plagued my mind. To make matters worse, running became more challenging as well.

I led the women's team as a freshman and sophomore. As a junior, my performance deteriorated as the breathing issues I struggled with in high school returned. It took everything in me to bring up the rear of our varsity team. Circumstances climaxed halfway through the year. My nutrient-deficient body literally put on the brakes. I limped off the track one afternoon after finishing an indoor meet. My body felt as though it was splitting in two. Shooting pain exploded through my pelvis with each step. Doctors conducted medical evaluations and MRIs. They pointedly informed me that I had multiple pelvic stress fractures.

"You're suffering from the female athlete triad," they told me. "Pelvic stress fractures are common in female athletes who overtrain, have a low BMI, and amenorrhea (absence of, or a missed menstruation after a normal menstrual cycle). You have all three. You need to take the next eight weeks off from running." I was devastated. I knew my body lacked nutrition. I realized I was underweight. I knew I was overtraining. I just didn't know how to self-correct. The doctors didn't offer much advice either. For those who've struggled with addiction, telling someone to "just change" doesn't work very well.

What was supposed to be an eight-week break turned into an eight-month sabbatical. During that time, every piece of my identity disintegrated. While I'd never wish my circumstances on anyone, my breaking point became my launching pad. I wish I could say my healing was instantaneous. It was not. Isn't it interesting how accepting deception takes only a moment, yet cultivating wholeness takes a lifetime? This was my reality.

Fortunately, my body healed by the time I started my senior year. I finished my college running career strong. Yet it would take another ten long years before peace enveloped my mind and spirit.

Before sinking into the depths of the disorder, my two greatest joys included eating meals with my loved ones and pushing my body to its limits. During the dark years of my life, these enjoyments became tainted. I couldn't fully engage with people because of the thoughts that constantly plagued my mind. I lost my enjoyment of running as it became a means to control my body. Over and over, I desperately sought the Lord for his mercy, grace, and healing. Slowly and gently, God began restoring my brokenness. He graciously revealed how even the darkness of my story could be transformed into something good.

One of my favorite songs is called "Fear is Not My Future" by Maverick City Music. The lyrics are an incredible declaration of truth! The first verse reminds me of what started to happen:

"Let Him turn it in your favor,
Watch Him work it for your good,
Cause He's not done with what He started,
He's not done until it's good"

In God's beautiful goodness, He began to take the fragments of my existence and gently piece them back together. He gave me beauty for my ashes, joyous blessing instead of mourning, and festive praise instead of despair (Isaiah 61:3).

My focus slowly shifted from my pain to the Person who knew me before I was born. During those years, I dove deeply into God's Word. I found Scriptures that declared the truth about who I was — who God created me to be. I spoke Philippians 1:6 (ESV), which says, "I am sure of this, that He who began a good work in you will bring it to completion at the day of Jesus Christ." I declared Psalm 139:14, "I will praise You because I am fearfully and wonderfully made." I believed Song of Songs 4:7, "You are altogether beautiful, my darling! There is no flaw in you!"

The Bible is sometimes called the Sword of the Spirit. I experienced the truth of this comparison. For many years, deception entangled my mind. However, when I started speaking God's Word over myself, it was as if a Sword slowly and powerfully cut away layer upon layer of lies. One day only Truth remained.

I discovered another powerful truth when I learned the meaning of my name. Growing up, my family and friends called me "Liz" or "Lizzy." I love my nickname as it brings back great memories from my childhood. However, after I married and moved to Colorado, I was determined to start my life as a new person. I asked people to call me Elizabeth. For me, it was a significant step in leaving the old me behind and beginning anew.

It was in Colorado that I discovered the meaning of my name. Elizabeth means "consecrated to God" and "God is abundance." This discovery was monumental. During my season of darkness, I would describe my life as being "consecrated to myself" and "living in lack." I'd been living a lie in direct contradiction to my name, and to who I was created to be. Isn't that where the enemy of our souls always tries to attack us? Doesn't he always target our identity?

Learning the truth of who I am positioned me within God's promise instead of within my pain. Now every time someone says my name, I imagine God singing His promises over me. He declares my value and worth! He gives life to the dead parts of my story! He creates new things out of nothing (Romans 4:17)! Lack of nutrition, lack of peace, and lack of freedom could no longer dominate. Through faith, I believed for abundance: abundant portion, abundant rest, and abundant liberty. And freedom finally broke through. No matter what your history, did you know that God promises to give you a new name (Revelation 2:17)? Does that propagate hope in you as it does in me?

My journey to wholeness and freedom was long. There were many days I wanted to give up. But God continually encouraged me along the way, miraculously working through people and resources. One specific encounter remains forever imprinted on my heart. I believe it serves as a gentle reminder of God's ever-present presence and incredible goodness.

Several months before we married, my husband, Isaac, excitedly accepted a job in Colorado Springs. He moved from New York to Colorado in April of 2004. He established a routine and made new friends. He had always wanted to live out West, so he felt thrilled about the move! We married in June, and I went west.

Contrary to his experience, the move to Colorado was a very difficult transition for me. I had no job, so I felt devoid of purpose. I had no family or friends, so I was beyond lonely. To make matters worse, I was still drowning in the depths of the eating disorder. My self-image was in shambles, and I questioned my value on a daily basis.

On one particularly challenging day, I left our apartment and walked to the nearby park. I just needed sunshine and fresh air. Both are abundant in Colorado! I walked and walked and walked. But I didn't even notice the beauty around me. I lamented to God, pouring out painful prayers from my heart. Nearing the end of my walk, I passed the park's playground. It was late in the afternoon, and the playground was devoid of children, quiet and alone. Alone. This was exactly how I felt. At that moment, I cried out in desperation, "God, can you please just show me how much you love me? Am I beautiful? Am I special? Do you even see me?!"

Immediately after I prayed that very emotionally desperate prayer, a little boy came running across the playground and started skipping alongside me. He seemed to be about four or five years old. Startled, since I thought the playground was empty, I wondered where this little boy came from. As I looked around, I noticed his parents far across the field sitting quietly at a picnic table.

I've always loved children, so I slowed my pace to match the little boy's gait. As he skipped alongside me, he started chattering away. "Do you know how much Jesus loves you?" The boy's first words pierced my aching heart. I was so surprised I nearly stopped in my tracks. The boy continued, "Jesus thinks you are special, and you are so beautiful!" With that, the child joyfully grinned up at me and said, "Bye!" He immediately ran off in the direction of his parents. I walked home that day in shock to God's immediate answer to my desperate prayer.

As I share this story, nearly twenty years later, tears of gratitude still course down my cheeks. I marvel at the loving heart of my Heavenly Father. Through the messenger of that angel-child, God beautifully orchestrated that very intimate encounter to demonstrate that He hears me. He loves me. He sees me. And He thinks I am beautiful.

My most powerful encounter with God came not on a mountaintop but during one of my lowest moments. At a time when I felt unknown. Devoid of purpose. Questioning my worth. It was here when I received the confirmation of my Father's love. Proving to me that He'll meet me where I am. That He values me when I'm not producing. That I'm beautiful just because I am His daughter.

Have you ever questioned your value, your worth? Do you ever wonder if anyone sees you? If anyone knows you? God says you are fearfully and wonderfully made (Psalm 139:14) and that nothing could ever separate you from His love (Romans 8:39). I grew up knowing these Scriptures. I had a personal relationship with Jesus. Yet these questions plagued my heart and mind. Honestly, sometimes they still do.

It's here that I feel compelled to point out another truth I rediscovered along this writing journey. Yes, I am called to live out my values — to live in community, to demonstrate compassion, to serve people, and to use my strengths to make the world a better place. Yet these values don't determine MY value. And they don't determine your value either. What you accomplish (or fail to accomplish) doesn't make you worthy (or unworthy). Your value is found in one truth alone. And that Truth is Jesus.

The little boy in the park joyfully proclaimed, "Do you know how much Jesus loves you?!" And I ask you the same question. "Do you know how much Jesus loves you?" For me, the park interaction solidified that God truly knows my thoughts, my moves, and my deepest insecurities. And He so gently meets me when I need Him most. He'll meet you when you need Him most too. No matter where that place is.

While I was editing my book, I stumbled upon a beautiful, ancient art form known as Kintsugi. This treasured 16th-century Japanese process mends broken pieces of pottery with gold, creating a new masterpiece out of something that could have been, maybe even should have been, discarded. Kintsugi artists behold and restore broken treasures, believing their new creation is even more valuable than the former. The restored pieces have lustrous golden seams that allow light to shine through.

When I learned about this incredible practice, my heart exploded with the truth of God's incredible redemption of His people. Isn't humanity broken? At times I feel undone by the magnitude of brokenness. Yet in the hands of *The Great Artist*, we are restored. We are recreated to become even more beautiful — not because we are now perfect and devoid of scars. Instead, we are more beautiful *because* of our brokenness! Just as Kintsugi pieces allow light to shine through, God reminded me that the same principle applies to my life. And yours. Despite our brokenness,

His beauty and light shine through our lives and into the lives of others.

Another Scripture that ministered to me throughout the restorative period of my life was Isaiah 43:18–19. It says, "Forget the former things; do not dwell on the past. See, I am doing a new thing! Now it springs up; do you not perceive it? I am making a way in the wilderness and streams in the wasteland." During that season, the former, painful things of my past were slowly put behind me as God's Truth propelled me forward. And Scripture is once again encouraging me through this season.

Are you waiting for the fulfillment of a promise? Overcoming an addiction? Trekking through a desert? If so, may I implore you to press into God's Word? And keep pressing, "I am sure of this, that He who began a good work in you will bring it to completion..." (Philippians 1:6).

I am reminded again of the song, "Fear Is Not My Future." These are the words of the bridge. It declares powerful promises for those of us who are in Christ:

"Fear is not my future, You are, You are!
Sickness is not my story, You are, You are!
Heartbreak is not my home, You are, You are!
Death is not the end, You are, You are!"

Isn't it magnificent that our fear, sickness, and heartache don't have to be all we ever know? We can find love, healing, and restoration in Christ!

Today, food and fitness have returned to their rightful places in my heart. They are no longer sources of pain and destruction, but are once again tools for connection and joy! I can delight again in preparing and hosting a meal around my family's table, offering others not only physical sustenance but a place to commune and belong. Running is again my favorite pastime. It has become a distinct part of my everyday routine. However, instead of using it to control my body, running is now a bridge to build relationships with others.

Most beautifully, my relationship with my twin sister, Laurel, is restored. In the fall of 2022, we celebrated our fortieth birthday. Throughout childhood and college, we celebrated every birthday together. Once I moved to Colorado, this practice ended. For the big 4-0, we decided to invest in a memory together. I invited Laurel and two of my dearest friends, Connilee and Ashlee, for a celebratory weekend in Colorado. They all joyfully accepted. I selected an invigorating trail half marathon. We raced together in style and wore matching crowns and capes! It was so much fun!

The single-track course was a mountainous series of ups and downs, twists and turns, and it demanded every ounce of our mental and physical strength. At most races, headphones are not allowed. Even so, when I race, songs often explode from my spirit into my mind. The mental music focuses my mind and helps my body settle into a pace. Especially when the songs are spiritual in nature. This happened at this race. Throughout the entire two-hour race, the song "Goodness of God" by Jenn Johnson, played through my being (sometimes there are benefits to the way my mind works).

"And all my life you have been faithful
And all my life you have been so, so good
With every breath that I am able
Oh, I will sing of the goodness of God

'Cause your goodness is running after, it's
running after me
Your goodness is running after, it's running after me
With my life laid down, I'm surrendered now
I give you everything
'Cause your goodness is running after, it keeps
running after me"

Up and down. Over rocks. Through mud. Across icy snow. We ran until we finished, all four of us within seconds of one another. We felt elated and humbly grateful for the abilities God had given us. Later that day, Laurel and I celebrated our victory at my favorite restaurant. We visited. We laughed. We ate. Together. Without any anxiety about the consequences of our rich meal. As we sat there, we cried grateful tears as we reflected on God's goodness and healing in our lives.

Several months later in June of 2023, Laurel and I reconnected in Millinocket. We enjoyed a commemorative time that was beyond anything we could have ever asked or imagined. We enjoyed many running explorations. We ran past our old high school track. We jogged through the thick woods around Stearns High School. We also discovered new recreational trails.

We also connected with our hometown pastor, Herschel Hafford. He asked us to sing and share at I Care Ministries. I played the piano, and we joyfully sang "Goodness of God." It remained my mantra the whole year after the race. I shared a brief synopsis of God's healing in my life. It was an incredibly special moment to realize that my journey had come full circle. I was back "home" in Millinocket where my values developed roots. It was also in Millinocket where I accepted seeds of deception. Where my blessings were exploited into burdens. Yet, as I sat there singing, I realized that my darkness had since transformed into light. God truly makes all things beautiful in His time.

In my current season, I coach my four children in the sport of running. All of my kids are incredible runners. I am excited to see what opportunities await them if they pursue this sport. I also enjoy cooking with my kids. We imaginatively explore recipes and culinary creations. I am excited to pass on my heritage of food and fitness while keeping both hobbies in their rightful place.

What heritage do you have? What pieces of your past shaped you into who you are today? Can you see God's masterpiece in the midst of your brokenness? Pensiveness can produce perspective — and peace — when viewed through the lens of a thankful heart. As you reflect on your journey, I hope you feel inspired to continue this day-by-day marathon we call "life."

I end this chapter with the lyrics to the song "Gratitude" by Brandon Lake, Benjamin Hastings, and Dante Bowe. These lyrics played throughout my spirit amidst this entire season of searching and reflecting. I feel so thankful for God's all-consuming, never-failing, always and forever faithful love.

All my words fall short
I got nothing new
How could I express
All my gratitude

I could sing these songs
As I often do
But every song must end
And you never do

So I throw up my hands
And praise you again and again
'Cause all that I have is a hallelujah
Hallelujah
And I know it's not much
But I've nothing else fit for a King
Except for a heart singing hallelujah
Hallelujah

So come on, my soul
Oh, don't you get shy on me
Lift up your song
'Cause you've got a lion inside of those lungs
Get up and praise the Lord

So, will you praise the Lord with me? Thank you for allowing me to share this piece of my journey. I pray you feel encouraged and empowered to continue in your own, beautifully unique story.

Rediscovering
COMMITMENT

Dear brothers and sisters, I don't mean to say that I have already achieved these things or that I have already reached perfection...But I focus on this one thing: Forgetting the past and looking forward to what lies ahead, I press on to reach the end of the race and receive the heavenly prize for which God, through Christ Jesus, is calling us.

— Philippians 3:13–14 (NLT)

The best use of your life
is to live your life so that the use of your life
outlives your life.

— Ron Puryear

One of my favorite classes in college was *Marriage and Family*. I find this ironic since my biology major required science and math courses, not social-emotional courses. I took the class as an elective and thoroughly enjoyed every aspect of it. Interestingly, though marriage and family are some of my top priorities today, I didn't write this chapter until I'd already finished the book. The truth is, I daily feel inadequate in my roles as a wife and mother. I'm still learning so much and don't feel qualified to share insight into these two very important, yet incredibly challenging, areas of life. Yet I felt the book was incomplete without a chapter celebrating children, marriage, and the compounding legacy of family. I decided to dive back into the experiences I had growing up. I will do my best to share what I learned from my parents about this. And I will humbly admit I do not have these areas figured out yet.

Throughout my early years, my parents reiterated that children are a gift from God. Family was a consistent topic of conversation. Mom often retold the miraculous accounts of each of our births. I grew up feeling thankful for the blessing of life. Mom has Type 1 Diabetes. Because of this, her pregnancies were challenging. Her pregnancy with Laurel and me was especially difficult. Mom developed toxemia at 27 weeks. Despite several weeks of bedrest, her condition did not resolve, so the doctors decided to deliver us early. In 1982 premature deliveries had much greater risks than they do today. The doctors prepared Dad and Mom for the worst. "Should it come down to saving Diane or saving the babies, on whom should we focus?" they asked. Dad and Mom wouldn't consider one over the other and firmly instructed, "Both." They then began praying Psalm 91 over the entire situation.

> "He who dwells in the shelter of the Most High,
> Will rest under the shadow of the Almighty.
> I will say of the Lord, "He is my refuge and my
> fortress, my God in whom I trust."
> He will cover you will His feathers,
> And under His wings you may seek refuge.
> No evil will befall you,
> Nor will any plague come near your tent.
> He will give His angels charge concerning you,
> To guard you in all your ways

With long life I (GOD) will satisfy you
And show you my salvation."
Psalm 91 (paraphrased)

Over and over, Mom and Dad prayed these promises.
Grandparents, aunts, uncles, and friends also agreed and
prayed for God's divine protection. Of course, my parents
felt frightened. Yet they stood strong in their faith, declaring
God's goodness despite the circumstances. Concerned for
the development of our lungs, the doctors waited until 32
weeks to deliver us. They administered drugs in utero to
enhance our lung growth. After our delivery, Laurel and
I stabilized in NICU. Miraculously, we were strong and
healthy despite our miniature size. We only needed several
weeks of NICU care before going home. Throughout my
childhood, Mom and Dad shared this miraculous story
over and over. I grew up understanding that children are
a blessing from the Lord. That I was a gift from God. As a
young girl, I adored babies and felt excited to have my own
family one day.

Mom's other pregnancies were much better. She
waited almost four years after our birth before having
Helene. Several years later, Amber and Seth were born
within sixteen months of each other. The doctors found
disturbing results with Seth's prenatal tests. The ultrasounds
showed kidney and brain abnormalities. No matter what
the findings, Mom and Dad were determined to deliver
him. Similar to Mom's pregnancy with Laurel and me, they
prayed Scripture over his developing body. Miraculously,

Seth was born without birth defects and was the most robust and active out of us all!

That's not to say that we didn't have any challenges after that. We did. Don't all families have obstacles to work through? Just before our move to Maine, Helene developed Type I Diabetes. She was only three years old at that time, and the years following her diagnosis required lifestyle modifications. These were the days before the invention of the convenient insulin pump. Mom checked Helene's blood sugar daily and administered insulin shots. She regulated the family diet to include routine snacks and balanced meals. Despite her discipline, she and Helene experienced occasional insulin reactions.

An insulin reaction occurs when a diabetic's blood sugar drops far below normal. Normal blood glucose levels may range between 70–140 mg/dL. When blood glucose levels drop below 50 mg/dL, an insulin reaction occurs. Every diabetic reacts differently to insulin reactions. The lower the blood sugar, the more severe the symptoms. Helene's severe lows always happened at night after everyone was sound asleep. This condition is called nocturnal hypoglycemia. Her first noticeable symptom involved screaming incoherently. She would wake up unaware of her surroundings and unable to communicate.

The first time this happened, she was only four years old. We had just moved to Maine and were living at the cabin on South Twin Lake. Mom and Dad didn't understand what was going on at first and thought Helene was having a nightmare. However, as Helene remained incoherent, Mom intuitively realized what was happening and began administering sugars to Helene's body. After Helene stabilized, my parents explained what transpired and taught us what to do if it happened again. At the time, Laurel and I were the only ones old enough to understand and help.

Throughout our childhood, Helene's nocturnal insulin reactions occurred several times each year. They came on without warning. Those nights were traumatic and frightening. I was sometimes asked to hold Helene's hand and console her while my parents worked to stabilize her body. I remember feeling helpless as I sat by her side and spoke words of comfort despite her incoherent state. Even though I knew she was going to be okay, uncontrollable tears often coursed down my cheeks. I felt overwhelming fear and pain seeing Helene in such a state. After an episode, it took much consolation and prayer for all of us to resume sleeping. Thankfully Helene came through all those experiences healthy and strong. I think those times cultivated empathy for those who can't help themselves. Despite the difficulties, my parents continuously blessed us with their words. They reiterated that we kids were their greatest gifts.

Both of my parents committed to raising us. However, I learned the most about family from my mother. Every day, it was my mom who exemplified sacrifice and selflessness. I've come to realize that both are essential for nurturing a family. As I mentioned before, Mom is one of the most capable people I know. Her daily discipline and grit are admired by many. She especially demonstrated an unparalleled resolve when serving her family.

Like many children, I didn't fully acknowledge or appreciate her dedication. Mom's intelligence earned her an accomplished degree in nursing. However, she decided to set her full-time career aside for several years and strategically focused on raising us. As mentioned earlier, Mom worked per diem at Millinocket Regional Hospital. She picked up shifts on evenings and weekends, arranging her schedule to prioritize the lives of her family. I found solace in knowing Mom would be home during the day.

Together, Mom and Dad decided she would be our primary influencer. Mom took the decision one step further and also committed to being our primary educator. She was often the first one awake in our home, cheerfully starting the insurmountable daily tasks before everyone else was up. Although I now know it wasn't easy on her, I rarely heard complaints escape her lips.

Sometimes, I sensed some days were more challenging for her than others. During these days, Mom's determination set in. She tackled her duties with quiet resolve, deciding to remain silent instead of spewing strife. As I mentioned in earlier chapters, Mom expected each of us to participate in the responsibilities of the home. She instilled the value of serving each other. "Many hands make light work," she often said. She cultivated an attitude of teamwork throughout our home, and liked to remind us that, "Families help each other out." This mindset remains with me to this day.

It was through Mom's example that I also intuitively observed the beautiful commitment of marriage. Mom and Dad share the same values and are both incredibly hard workers. But their personalities are totally opposite. Mom is structured, disciplined, contemplative, practical, and energized. I don't know too many people who get more done in a single day than my mom. She can disassociate from her emotions and commit to processes and procedures in order to accomplish a result. She can fall in love with the mundane, knowing that her daily discipline will produce a great reward. Mom gets excited about planning for events weeks in advance, and she prefers to stick to her plan.

On the other hand, Dad is spontaneous, generous, tenderhearted, creative, and easygoing. Always willing to try something new, Dad's adventurous spirit led our family to move multiple times, start multiple businesses, and freely adapt from one season to the next. Dad does not necessarily need to finish what he starts. Plans impede Dad's spontaneity. He calmly "goes with the flow" — even if he doesn't know where that flow is going to end up! Relaxed about life, Dad's resilience is something I admire. He bounces back quickly even when circumstances don't end up as expected.

Despite their differences, they committed to each other from the start. As a child, I felt security knowing Mom and Dad would stay married. My parents edified one another in front of us kids. They verbally built each other up in their strengths and didn't focus on their weaknesses. Dad supported Mom, and Mom supported Dad. They worked together as a team and didn't compete with each other. As an adult, I admire their marriage. I asked Mom what helped her with her marriage. Mom humbly conveyed her challenges as a young wife.

"I realized shortly after I married your father that there were a lot of habits and tendencies that I didn't know about. I quickly understood why many couples choose to divorce one another, and I even briefly thought about that option. However, I realized that if I had married someone else, or if I chose to leave your dad, then I would have a completely different set of challenges. Frustrations and hardships wouldn't disappear with another husband. I'd still have them because we're all human. We're all different, and we all have areas that irritate one another. So, I could either choose to magnify your father's weaknesses by criticizing him and tearing him down. Or, I could choose to focus on your father's strengths, overlook our differences, and decide to make the best of our relationship."

And they did make the best of their relationship. In front of us, Dad frequently flirted with Mom. He purposefully interrupted whatever she was doing to shower her with affection or compliments. Mom continuously praised Dad. She edified his efforts to provide for our family through his creative pursuits. It was a beautiful partnership to witness. I feel grateful I grew up with their example.

My parents are now over forty-five years into their marriage journey. They both tell me it is more satisfying and fulfilling than it's ever been. I recently asked Mom about her feelings about following Dad to Maine and later on to other states, each time pursuing different opportunities. My mother's response was full of grace and honor. She helped me realize why their marriage continues to flourish. She said,

"Elizabeth, your father is a dreamer, a visionary. When he has new ideas, he's full of excitement and life. I've learned over the years that it's better for me to support him in his dreams than to try to dampen his desires. Even if his plans fail, and sometimes they do, I'd rather give him the flexibility to be creative and excited about his future. When I try to control his ideas, I stifle his spirit."

Mom's wisdom is amazing. I still have a lot to learn in the area of marriage. Mom's response coincides well with how my mentors answered a similar question. They've been married for nearly thirty years. I recently asked them what contributed to their marriage success. "We have mutual respect in our marriage," they said. "We give each other grace to run in our own lane. And edification. We edify each other frequently. Edification unifies; criticism divides."

Mom and Dad's example magnified the attractiveness of marriage and family. Even as a teenager, I felt excited to embark on that journey. I met my incredible husband, Isaac, on the cross-country team as a freshman in college. We immediately had the commonality of faith and both enjoyed outdoorsy, athletic activities. I initially thought we were similar. Yet I soon found out our similarities were quite limited! I discovered the saying "opposites attract" to be unequivocally true. I still find it fascinating how relational differences seem to be magnetic.

Isaac and I decided to marry right after college. We began our lifetime adventure on June 19, 2004. As I'm editing this book, we are heading into our twentieth year of marriage. It has definitely been a journey! As most young people are, I was naive to the dedication and commitment our marriage relationship would require. I thought we worked through most of our challenges during our four-year courtship. We had the privilege of spending every day together. We participated in cross-country and track practices. We traveled as teammates around the country. We witnessed how we handled stressors and victories. Because we knew each other so well, our first seven years of marriage were relatively *easy* compared to what most couples experience.

It's been the last thirteen years of raising a family that has brought *hundreds*, if not *thousands*, of opportunities to work through conflict and challenges. We intentionally waited for many years before starting our family, yet when we finally decided to have kids, we did so rapidly. We had four children in six years. In case you are wondering, we joyfully planned each child!

Growing up in a large close-knit family developed my heart for motherhood. Always ready for a challenge, I desired a large family. Naturally maternal, I loved every minute of the baby phase. Like most mothers, I not only felt indescribable love toward my babies, but fierce protection. Andrew, Charis, Wyatt, and Liam are my life's biggest blessings. I continually feel a mixture of excitement and responsibility as I nurture them.

However, my parenting ideals and maternal moments came to a crashing halt once my beloved Andrew turned three. He is my oldest child. Andrew is the most strong-willed, determined child I've ever met. *How do I parent this incredibly energetic little human being*? I wondered. By the time I'd had my fourth little blessing, I was in over my head. I identified with the comedian, Jim Gaffigan. His spoof on raising kids articulates a conversation between an onlooker and himself.

Onlooker, incredulously comments, "So...you have four kids...four?!"

"Yes," sighs Jim. "I have four."

"Oh..." the Onlooker raises his eyebrows in a dubious expression. "What's that like?"

Jim sighs again and thoughtfully contemplates what to say. "Well," he begins, "Imagine you're drowning, and someone hands you a baby..."

The dialogue is hilarious. It is also frighteningly accurate. I often felt as though I were drowning. Every day. For about ten years. Then there were the times I received interesting comments from people while I was out and about. Even when they were little, my kids came with me on errands. Many people smiled at me sympathetically and said, "Wow, you've got your hands full." As if I didn't already realize that as I was trying to finagle four young children and groceries throughout the store without having a panic attack. Some would go one step further and ask my kids' ages. Once I told them, they'd nod knowingly and say, "Oohhh, girl, you're IN it..." as if I was supposed to know what that meant. *IN* it ...*in* trouble, *in* conflict, *in* chaos...*in over my head*? I wasn't quite sure what I was IN, but I knew I was IN something. Something I didn't quite anticipate or know how to handle.

Not only do I have four children, but three of them are boys. I grew up in a family of five kids but the four oldest are girls. Can I say that's a very different dynamic than boys? People wonder why I get up at 4:30 a.m. and how I can stay committed to running every morning. Let me tell you...it is the *only* solitude I am guaranteed in a twenty-four-hour period. My husband jokes with others that he gladly supports my morning habit because it's cheaper than therapy!

Gone are my ideals of reading quietly to my children around the fire on cold, winter afternoons. We've tried, and inevitably a weapon comes out from somewhere and whacks an unsuspecting sibling on an exposed body part. Despite my daily reminders, *and consequences*, my couches aren't used for sitting. They're launching pads for adventures that should only take place outdoors. And it doesn't matter if I confiscate all the Nerf guns and swords. My decorative couch pillows become weapons of mass destruction as my boys test their mighty strength with one another, pummeling each other until someone ends up crying.

Then, there's mealtime. I envisioned long conversations around the table, enjoying delicious meals of homemade soup and bread. What's materialized is quite different. Most of the time I'm independently trying to maintain some semblance of order as my husband frequently works late. Suppertime consists of encouraging my sons to keep their bottoms in their chairs and the chair's legs on the ground. At the same time, I find myself reminding them that noises that imitate bodily functions should be kept in the bathroom and not at the dining room table. During their earlier years, there was always at least one child who spilled his water or (somehow) fell out of his chair. To my silence-loving, introverted self, mealtimes felt just short of embarking on the beaches of Normandy.

Throughout these chaotic years, I found myself asking, *why did I voluntarily choose the life of family?* It sure didn't look like my growing-up years. I felt clueless about how to make it all work! I am still amazed at the destruction that takes place on a daily basis. There was one season I now recall with fondness when all four of my children were under the age of six. My oldest son is shrewdly devious. Andrew's delight in each day is magnetic. He has more energy than any human being should be allowed to have. Every day then (and now) brought lots of excitement — and some unexpected challenges.

In the spring of 2018, we'd just finished having our van windows replaced. Andrew haplessly shattered them. He was playing with handfuls of rocks when he started jubilantly twirling around and around. He nonchalantly allowed the centrifugal force to pull the rocks from his hands. The rocks showered in all directions. The only problem was our van. It sat idly in the driveway and received the brunt of the rock shower. I discovered the true meaning of shatter that day. Fragments of the van window exploded all about the vehicle. It was shortly thereafter we had another accident involving shards of glass.

At the time we lived in a cozy, century-old bungalow. Although updated, it maintained beautiful craftsman architecture throughout the home. The front door was an antique and contained beautifully crafted four-foot panes of glass amidst delicate wooden trim. It was just another ordinary day when Andrew decided to play a game. He recruited his four-year-old sister, Charis, to join him. They discovered great fun running down the short hallway between the dining and living room. Their new game involved body-slamming the front door. I am sure you can see where this is going.

I was in our galley kitchen when I heard a banging noise. I peeked my head through the doorway to see what could be making such a ruckus. Just as I raised my voice in admonition, I watched in horror as Andrew's and Charis' bodies slammed through the door, dispersing shards of glass on either side of the entryway. Thankfully both kids were unharmed. After my husband returned home, he voiced his frustration. "How can so many accidents happen when you are less than thirty feet away?" I often wondered the same thing.

It was in this season that more than just glass shattered. The stability of family as I knew it fragmented in more than one way. Have you had seasons of continued upheaval? They are not easy.

In 2018, my youngest sister, Amber, had a life-altering brain hemorrhage. She miraculously survived. Yet the weeks, months, and years following her incident were some of the most challenging I've ever experienced. I was thousands of miles away from most of the trauma but the grief and pain were very near. Then, while Amber was still recovering, a tragic car accident killed one of my cousins.

As I was wading through these waves of grief, my foundation was shaken even more. Quite unexpectedly my husband asked if we could start marriage therapy. We'd been navigating little misunderstandings for close to a decade, yet many issues remained. What began as a single session turned into two years of counseling. We peeled back layer upon layer of misunderstanding, unmet expectations, and pain. Paired with the grief of my sister's condition, I frequently felt overcome with despondency. I often didn't want to continue on the path of family.

I hope my frank honesty is not repelling but realistically relatable. I understand why so many throw themselves into their careers instead of their families. It sure seems temporarily more rewarding. Being a wife and mother is not measurable. I don't frequently receive praise from my children. Pats on the back are few and far between. My house looks like a disaster. Siblings fight with one another. And I lose my patience with my husband and my kids. I fight feelings of failure day in and day out. I often feel frenetic, and the thoughts that run through my head frighten me at times. Have you ever been there?

Because I participated in running a household as a child, I felt somewhat prepared for the amount of physical work that was required. Washing laundry, cleaning the house, and meal prep were nearly second nature to me. Yet I felt ill-equipped for the emotional strain that came with my parenting and wifely duties. What does it look like to disciple and discipline my strong-willed yet sensitive children? How do I honor my husband despite the myriad of unmet expectations? Many times, I truly do not know what to do. I daily look to Jesus for help and implement the advice of those I admire.

One of my mentors challenges me (in a good way) by saying, "Don't get offended. If you get offended easily, don't get married, don't have kids, and don't do anything great." While he jokingly offers this advice with a smile, I find so much truth in his words. I must admit I am sensitive. And

I am easily offended. Yet here I find myself — married, with kids, and in pursuit of greatness. Guarding my heart from disappointment is not something I ever thought to prepare for. This is where I found myself at the onset of this book. Not only did I feel disappointed vocationally, but I felt disillusioned with the relationships of my family. I just didn't know it was going to be this hard. What about you? Are you feeling disappointment in your career? In your marriage? In your family?

A server by nature, I thought I was cut out for the role of wife and mother. By default, I discovered many things about myself that I didn't previously know. Things like how opinionated, idealistic, and emotionally unstable I can be (those of you who know me well probably already knew these things, but raising a young family opened my eyes to my overwhelming shortcomings). I am realizing that some of my ideals set me up for *daily* disappointment. My expectations are often unrealistic. The season of family brings the most beautiful joy but also delivers gut-wrenching pain. To say these past thirteen years have been a growth journey would be the understatement of the decade. It's only by God's grace that I am still persevering and choosing commitment over comfort.

I also feel discouragement, and sometimes anger, as I watch people I love separate and divorce. Sometimes I question my decision to stay committed. At times I am tempted to follow their lead and choose what *appears to be* the easy way out.

Can I get out of the commotion and conflict? I wonder. *Don't I deserve more than the hand that I've been dealt?* These questions — *these lies* — have plagued my heart and mind more frequently than I'd like to admit.

I am finding respite in the gentle counsel of God's Word. My mom continually encourages me with her wisdom and grace. Mentors consistently challenge me to seek truth and walk it out. I haven't figured out all the answers, but humbly contemplate the beauty of commitment. May I share my thoughts with you?

First of all, if you've chosen to separate or divorce, there's no condemnation, only understanding and grace. I relate to the many challenges that accompany the beautiful yet messy ministry called marriage. I will not pretend to understand all of the pain that you have experienced. And some situations demand separation. Sometimes marriage partners must seek safety away from an abusive spouse. I understand this.

For those in functional marriages, I implore you to keep going. I watch my parents as they are enjoying their years as empty nesters. Their example propagates faith and optimism that persevering will be worth it. Ultimately, it's their commitment to each other and their family that birthed this book. It's *their legacy* that I've written about. And it's their legacy that I desire to pass on. Dad sometimes feels despondent over not leaving more of a legacy *for* us kids. Yet I couldn't disagree more. Dad and Mom have left a legacy *in* each of us. It continues to live on through our commitment to our values. And family is one of those values.

In a recent conversation with my mom, she encouraged me to focus on my husband's strengths. I know enough not to run to Mom with my sob stories of how challenging my marriage is. Mom offers empathy but doesn't provide a place for me to wallow in self-pity. She doesn't minimize the mess. She just consistently and firmly reminds me to fix my eyes on the future, the prize, the finish line. Mom's perspective reminds me of something my husband recently spoke to me about.

Isaac and I were lamenting over yet another friend who decided to leave their spouse. I empathized with their situation and commented on the dysfunction I see all around me.

"Don't you ever want to walk away?" I asked, knowing my own frequent desires to depart from the difficult.

"Well, those thoughts have come, but I don't entertain them." Isaac's answer surprised and challenged me. His resolve reminded me of my mom. Isaac experiences frustration and irritation with me just as I do with him. Yet he maintains an emotional stability that I have yet to learn. Have you learned emotional stability yet?

He continued, "Elizabeth, we're in the middle of the race. Isn't the middle of the race always the hardest? It's there that most let off the gas, contemplate quitting, and often give up. It's in the middle of the race when you can't see the end, when you wonder if the finish line is actually up ahead, if finishing will even be worth it. You're already hurting yet you know there's still additional discomfort up ahead. Isn't the middle the most painful part? We're *IN* that part right now. We've got to keep our faith. The finish line will be worth it."

The finish line will be worth it.

I am learning to celebrate little victories. As I write this chapter, my kids are 12, 10, 8, and 6. They can now put on their shoes independently (mostly), buckle themselves in and out of their car seats, sleep through the night (most nights), and go to the bathroom by themselves. I've also seen glimpses of empathy, compassion, and discipline begin to blossom in their character.

It's a new season, and I am embarking on another journey of growth. I am sure this season will have its own set of victories. And its own set of challenges. However, I am learning to reject the lies that my success as a mother occurs only when my kids are compliant and controlled, that fulfillment in my marriage only materializes when my needs are met and my husband is satisfied. Ultimately, my sole satisfaction must stem out of my relationship with Jesus, not out of that with my children or my spouse. It's a lesson that continues to resurface in my life. Over and over. What about you? Where are you finding your satisfaction? Your fulfillment?

As I mentioned before, I am an idealistic person. I've come to realize I need to put some of my ideals to rest — let them go as they have stolen many days, weeks, months, and years of joy. I am not saying I've given up on my life, but I am considering the source of my contentment.

In his book *The Ruthless Elimination of Hurry*, John Mark Comer writes, "Contentment isn't some Buddhist-like negation of all desire; it's living in such a way that your unfulfilled desires no longer curb your happiness. We all live with unfulfilled desires. In this life, all our symphonies remain unfinished. But this doesn't mean we can't live happy."

His summary of contentment pretty much sums up this season of life. I am learning to live with joy and contentment despite my unfulfilled desires. I choose to embrace this season — this life I find myself in. It's full of chaos, noise, needs, and unmet expectations. It's also overflowing with joy, laughter, life, and — if I so choose — contentment.

Reflecting on the beginning of the chapter and the promises of Psalm 91, I am reminded that my satisfaction can rest on the One who created me. Toward the end of the passage, God says, "With long life I will satisfy him and show him my salvation." If I am looking for satisfaction, joy, peace, or contentment in anyone other than my Heavenly Father, I will come up empty every time. He alone is the Creator of my life. He alone is the author of my story. He alone is the source of my satisfaction. And He can be your source, too.

The finish line will be worth it. Isaac's words still echo through my mind. I'll be honest, I sometimes have doubts. Yet no matter the outcome, whether it's pretty or painful, I've decided to finish. I choose faith over frustration and encouragement instead of criticism. I will focus on the future prize instead of the present problems. Will you join me?

As I close this chapter, I want to share a poem that Dad wrote back in 2017. It beautifully articulates his perspective of his family. I share it with you as I think it perfectly illustrates the brevity of life as well as the reality of the finish line.

The Finish Line

I'm past my prime,
Looking at the finish line.
I must confess,
My life's been blessed.

Before my prime, I took my time,
Thinking it would never end.
Family time went by so fast,
That part of life, just a flash.

Now they're gone, we stay in touch.
Don't see them nearly enough.
Grandkids now and easy chairs,
Look out windows with long stares.

The setting sun with reddish skies,
I feel the wetness in my eyes.
I think of toys and noise, on my lap wiggles.
My little girls, with laughs and giggles.

A son that asked so many questions,
Now has answers, not to mention.
The future's bright for my crew of five.
Their mom, the crown jewel in my eyes.

I'm past my prime, blessed beyond measure.
The final stretch, a time to treasure.
Can no longer sprint, I'll take my time,
Walking to the finish line.

Rediscovering
THE WAY HOME

Commit to the Lord whatever you do,
and He will establish your path.

— Proverbs 16:3 (NIV)

Life is God's novel.

Let Him write it.

— Isaac Bashevis Singer

Proverbs 16:3 basically sums up the whole book. Dad reminds me of this verse often. "Keep God at the center of your life, Lizzy, and He will direct your path." It was the quote I used for my senior yearbook. It's resurfaced throughout my adult life. And it came up again recently. As I write this chapter, I am sitting in the airport ready to board another plane. Traveling westward from Maine back to Colorado. The spur-of-the-moment trip solidified several things. Like how I can experience miracles within simple moments. How God's purpose for my life is often bigger than my plan. How God will meet me where I am. Even if I'm in the middle of nowhere!

I left Millinocket 23 years ago. It's been just as long since I spent any significant time there. I relocated for college in 2000. Due to another career change, Dad moved the family away from Maine in 2001. Since then, I've only been back a few times.

It's amazing how my week in Maine came to pass. Dad likes to fish in Maine every year. In 2023, he offered the trip to several of his grandkids, my oldest son included. Dad planned for mid-June. So earlier that spring, I researched flights and travel options for Andrew. Andrew was 11 years old at the time which meant he had to be accompanied. This created limited travel options and incurred additional fees.

That's when an idea started forming in my mind — what if I could go, too? Maybe I could fly to Maine with Andrew and stay in Millinocket while the boys fished? How fun would it be to visit Maine while editing my book? Maybe I could have several days to myself. Carve out some quiet time to write and think. Enjoy some peace.

Initially I pushed my desires aside. I talked myself out of my idea. *Who will take care of my other three children,* I wondered. *How selfish — expecting Isaac to complete his job AND take care of the kids*? I internally wrestled with all of these questions before communicating my desires out loud.

I finally expressed what I was thinking to Isaac during one of our dates. As we hiked through the beautiful trails of Red Rocks Open Space, I burst into tears. That spring brought with it a whirlwind of activity, change, and drama. I was at the end of myself. Again. Isaac gently asked me what I needed to get my head in the right space. I expressed my desire to get away — by myself. I shared my thoughts about escaping to Maine. Isaac totally surprised me with his answer.

"I think you should go," he commented.

"What?!" I exclaimed. "Who will take care of the kids while I am away?"

Isaac graciously volunteered to work from home for the week of our trip. "I'll figure it out," he said.

I couldn't believe my ears.

"Really?" I asked, doubtful he was being serious. "Are you sure you want to take on both work and the kids for a whole week — on your own?" My husband is an extremely capable man. However, he'd never combined work and parenting for such an extended time. I was nervous that he truly didn't comprehend what he volunteered to do. He simply, and calmly, reiterated that he would figure it out.

After I recovered from the shock, excitement began to build. I couldn't even fathom a whole week away! I couldn't remember the last time I was alone for more than several hours. And Millinocket of all places?! To say I was ecstatic would be a grand understatement! I immediately told my sister, Laurel, about my plans. She shared my excitement and asked if she could join me for several days. I quickly agreed. Laurel considerately planned her trip for the latter half of my stay, accommodating my desire for some alone time.

Throughout the early weeks of June, the mental and emotional fog I'd experienced for the past six months started to clear. My energy and optimism also began to return. I traveled to Maine feeling better than I had in months. Questions still lingered in my mind. I had so many different endeavors. Which ones should I pursue, and which ones should I let go? I also felt unsettled about my travel plans. I am a flexible person, yet I find peace in having a plan. Plans give me a sense of purpose. Entering my trip, I didn't have either.

As I mentioned in an earlier chapter, I haven't kept in touch with many Maine friends. My list of people to reconnect with was short. *Who still lives in the area?* I wondered. *What activities will I enjoy while I'm away?* Questions without answers fired rapidly through my mind, and I tried to turn them off. I looked forward to relaxing, but I knew I wouldn't be able to sit around the whole week. I like to be active in solitude.

The entire trip ended up being nothing like I'd envisioned. Yet it couldn't have been better if I'd expertly planned every moment. From the time I arrived in Maine, a feeling of expectation filled my heart. I had a hunch my trip promised more than I expected.

Things started to unfold with the rental car. I had excitedly booked the most compact car available. I was ready for something speedy and small — something other than a "mom car." But the day I arrived in Portland, all the compact cars were gone. The rental car salesman apologized and asked if I would accept a van.

Perhaps the upgraded size would have been welcomed by others, but I immediately felt disappointed. I am not opposed to minivans. I spent many years driving these practical, family vehicles. I love big vehicles and currently drive an oversized Suburban. It just wasn't what I had planned.

I checked my attitude, yet I still felt unusually let down. Even slightly irritated. On the outside, I accepted his suggestion with a smile, yet I internally questioned the change of plans. *Is there a greater purpose to this alternative vehicle, or is this just a test of my attitude?* I wondered. I would not fully understand the reason for the van until the last day of my trip.

As Andrew and I drove through Portland, I marveled at the serene atmosphere. It was so different from Colorado Springs. I once thought Portland was a booming metropolis. Now I saw it was quaint and quiet. That peaceful welcome set the stage for the remainder of my visit.

I headed north to Greenville. Dad, my nephews, and Dad's friends had arrived several days earlier and already set up camp. We planned to meet them and leave Andrew with them for the next several days. I cherished the three-hour drive and marveled at the peaceful beauty surrounding me. Just as I remembered, there were very few people or cars along the highway. The only abundant commodities were wild lupines, thick forests, and bugs. Oh yes, there were lots of bugs! Ticks, mosquitoes, and black flies bombarded us. After picking off several ticks and slapping away biting mosquitoes, I had the startling realization that I forgot to pack bug spray! I realized then that I've become accustomed to the high desert of Colorado Springs where bugs are basically non-existent.

Our time in Greenville was brief. After meeting up with Dad, he informed me that the fishing wasn't great. "Would you consider taking the boys to Millinocket with you tomorrow?" he asked me. "I'd like to fish one more day with my friends, but I don't think the boys will enjoy fishing here. It's been unusually slow. I'll join you in Millinocket in several days. What do you think?" Wanting everyone to be happy, I consented. I realized my trip wasn't going to be quite the quiet getaway I'd anticipated. It was turning out to be something else altogether. I wondered what other changes might be in store throughout the remainder of my time.

When I woke up the next morning, I felt as though I'd stepped back in time. Greenville is not Millinocket, but the atmosphere is similar. That first morning, Dad and I had an interesting conversation with the motel manager. The friendly woman greeted us as we were about to depart for our fishing adventure. I anticipated a brief hello. I couldn't have been more wrong. Our hello turned into a 30-minute conversation. The manager was so friendly, inquisitive, and kind. Her generosity and care immediately reminded me of the community that first welcomed my family to Millinocket.

The friendly welcome quickly turned into a comical conversation. She and Dad exchanged stories about house keys — or lack thereof. Dad informed the woman that during the family's years in Millinocket, we'd never owned a house key. Anytime we traveled away from town, we locked the front door but the back door remained open. The manager related to this and shared stories of a similar situation.

"I have to be extra careful when I have guests from out of state!" she commented. "They automatically lock my doors!" At this, the lady gasped as if she was incredulous that people would intuitively do such a thing. I felt right at home as she continued, "If I happen to leave the house before they do, I need to watch out! I may never get back in!" The manager giggled and then lowered her voice as if letting us in on a secret. "In fact, I don't know if I've ever had a key to my house!"

We all laughed at the story. Of course, not everyone in northern Maine applies the same mindset toward locking their homes. But the interaction reminded me of the uniqueness of my childhood. Nostalgia set in as I contemplated the unadulterated trust and goodwill that Mainers have for one another. How beautiful it is to enjoy the simplicity of life and relationships without fear of harm. How could I cultivate this in the big city? I tucked the conversation away into the recesses of my heart and determined to treat people with this kind of trust and goodwill even after I returned to Colorado.

The remainder of the morning included a special fishing outing with my dad. I even caught a beautiful trout! It had been years since I fished with Dad. Sitting with him in the canoe brought back so many wonderful memories. We later enjoyed delicious trout for brunch. It was the sweetest trout I had ever eaten, and so vibrantly colored that it looked artificial! The memories from that special morning will remain imprinted on my mind for years to come.

The boys and I loaded into the van and drove on to Millinocket. I found many aspects of town vastly different from what I remembered. I entered from the west side, driving by my Knox Street home and the once-active paper mill. I immediately noticed some changes. The mill's smokestacks stood empty, nearly forgotten. The once clamorous train tracks, which for decades carried thousands of tons of lumber, stood quiet. Overgrown grass waved along the tracks as if gently declaring the demise of the tired town. As

I circled through those familiar streets, gone were many of the meticulously kept homes and yards. Some houses stood distressed, and many lots were in disarray. There were even vacant lots where abandoned houses had been torn down. I took many deep breaths to keep my emotions in check.

Continuing through town, my initial stop was a sentimental one — the Stearns High School Track. This was where I'd discovered my love for running. The track itself looked as if it hadn't been used since I left 23 years before. Yet the stadium still stood proud overlooking the football field. My son and nephews ran a victory lap. I watched from the stands, overcome with mixed emotions.

I felt apprehension as reality set in. So many sights were different. Quieter than I remembered. Worn out. Yet, I also felt curiosity. What had stayed the same? And was there anything new? At that moment I felt thankful to have the company of my son and nephews. Their youthful energy provided a welcome distraction amidst the tumultuous emotions that left my heart reeling.

The following days provided answers to my curiosity. Yes, the town's vibrancy was not what it once was. So many people suffered extensively and moved on when the mill shut its doors over 15 years before. Yet the hearts of those who stayed were just as welcoming as they had been before.

I had anticipated a quiet, solitary time away. Instead, the days turned into vibrant times of connection. I stayed with Debbi Perkins. Remember Debbi? She's the one who helped Mom remodel our house. Who took Laurel and me back-to-school shopping. A great family friend. She and I enjoyed many beautiful conversations. I saw old neighbors, classmates, and friends — people I hadn't seen for over 20 years. I met others who were complete strangers. No matter if the connection involved a long-lost companion or a new-found friend, I was welcomed and embraced. Similar to my interaction with the motel manager in Greenville, five-minute hellos turned into 30-minute conversations.

Time seemed to tick by slower in this treasured town. Neighbors still cared for each other. People still poured into one another. They joined forces to rebuild their town. New businesses and community initiatives added value. My heart felt overwhelmed by my discoveries.

The time in Maine felt divinely orchestrated in every way. Each day held God-ordained interactions, one right after the other. I acquired so many new memories. These special times will continue to remind me of God's gentle direction. A thin thread seemed to connect my previous life with my current. One of the most impactful interactions occurred after my twin sister, Laurel, arrived.

Laurel flew to Maine several days after me. I picked her up from Bangor International Airport, and we started making memories together. It was a rainy afternoon when Laurel and I visited many special people. We toured our old home. Our previous neighbors, Randy and Anne Jackson, purchased and renovated the property. The finished product was beautiful. I felt joy as I thought about these dear people living in my childhood home. We discovered our other neighbors remained the same as well. We knocked on their doors and introduced ourselves. In typical Maine fashion, they welcomed us. We leisurely visited on their doorstep.

The entire evening was lovely. As we got ready to leave, we thought our afternoon of visiting was complete.

When we pulled away from the Jackson's house, I thought about Mr. Hartwell, the man who mentored Laurel and me in horsemanship. Who allowed us to help him with his horses. Who purchased us our very first tack. Who gave us his barn when we received Kedar. In typical twin fashion, Laurel voiced my thoughts. "Do you think Mr. Hartwell still lives down the street?" I laughed and said, "I was thinking the very same thing," We started driving in the direction of his house. As I considered our dear friend, my heart began to patter nervously.

"Do you think Mr. Hartwell and his wife are even still alive?" Laurel wondered.

"Well, let's stop by and find out!" I replied.

We drove the two blocks to the end of Knox Street.

When we arrived, everything looked the same. I again felt as though I'd stepped back in time. Laurel jumped out of the van and ran up to the front door. She knocked, and Mrs. Hartwell answered. Laurel excitedly stumbled over her words as she explained who she was. It took Mrs. Hartwell a brief minute to get over her shock at who was standing on her doorstep.

"Is Mr. Hartwell here, too?" Laurel asked. Mrs. Hartwell recovered from her shock and invited us into their enclosed porch. "Yes, he's here!" she answered and briefly departed to gather her husband. "You've got to come see who's here!" I heard her call through the kitchen. Mrs. Hartwell didn't reveal our names.

Mr. Hartwell quietly walked onto the porch and stood there, his eyes searching our faces. Recognition quickly registered. "Laurel and Liz?" He questioned. We joyfully nodded and embraced our dear friend. Overwhelming emotions flooded our hearts from our unexpected reunion. Joyful tears ran down all of our faces.

We enjoyed such a lovely visit on the porch that evening. We updated each other on our lives. We laughed at old memories. We shared about our families. And, of course, we talked about horses. Several months earlier I'd written about Mr. Hartwell as I recounted the story of my horse. I didn't think then that I would ever see him again. I didn't know I would get the chance to thank him, and to let him know what an impact he'd made on me. But on the front porch that day, Laurel and I had the opportunity to personally thank Mr. Hartwell — for everything. It was incredible.

We discovered the Hovel had been dismantled and leveled in 2018 due to township changes. Horses are no longer allowed on Millinocket's leased land. I visited the site. True to Mr. Hartwell's description, the hovel bears no remnants of what I remember. All the barns are gone. Only trees and grass remain. No matter what, I will always gratefully remember the many miracles that happened there. Largely due to the God-given friendship of Mr. Hartwell.

Earlier in this chapter, I mentioned arriving in Millinocket with questions about the direction of my life. I held those questions loosely. *Will I find answers in this remote wilderness?* I wondered. I didn't think so. It felt too far away. Too removed from my present life to gain any direction for the future.

Miraculously, most of my questions were answered. In the far-removed forests of Maine, God once again reminded me that He's faithfully involved in every detail of my life. My location doesn't matter to Him. Remember my Colorado park story when God spoke to me through the angel child? After an encounter like that, why did I doubt He could do it again? Maybe because I'm human. Do you ever think God won't come through for you again, even if He did it before? Well, God did speak to me again. Ironically this time it was through an elderly gentleman at I Care Ministries.

Still served faithfully by Herschel Hafford, ICM maintains its community outreach during weekdays. Herschel also continues a small Sunday service. Before traveling to Maine, I notified Herschel about my visit. He requested Laurel and I sing during the Sunday service, and we agreed.

I still don't like performing in front of others. But when I do, I prayerfully consider what to play. The theme of gratitude seemed to resurface all year, so I chose "Goodness of God" by Jenn Johnson. It's the same song that played through my heart when Laurel and I ran together for our fortieth birthday.

Because I play most music by ear, I don't have any sheet music. Yet when I play in front of others, nerves make my insides shake so badly that I sometimes forget everything I know! So, when I perform, I prefer to have chord progressions and lyrics in front of me. But I forgot to find the chords for the song. When I arrived at Debbi's house, I discovered that very song, complete with chord progressions, sitting on her piano stand. I used the chords for reference that Sunday. It was like a little gift from above.

More of these little gifts started to accumulate. When Laurel and I arrived for the service, Herschel told us that he selected only one song to play that Sunday. Guess which song it was? You guessed it — "Goodness of God" by Jenn Johnson. Herschel didn't know we'd planned the very same song and was overjoyed to discover our choice. This small moment gave me peace. It confirmed that God is truly aware of my little plans. When I am sensitive to His lead, my plans fit into His larger purpose.

There were less than 20 attendees that Sunday. One couple were special guests from out of town. Herschel scheduled the couple's visit months in advance. The gentleman intended to share special music that Sunday. As I talked with them, I felt struck by their kindness and love. The gentleman seemed close to the age of my Nana.

As I mentioned, I was still navigating a tumultuous season seeking direction with my endeavors. One project in particular was taking more time and effort than I expected. It seemed like it had the promise of a long-lasting positive impact and could be incredibly successful, but I felt weary of it. I had been asking myself every day, *Is this project the best use of my time and resources?* As I talked with the gentleman further, I discovered he had incredible success — and lasting impact — with a similar endeavor 50 years before. He even knew the developers of my pursuit and only had positive things to say about them. He encouraged me and gently confirmed that I was on the right track.

That conversation left my head reeling. *Did that connection really just happen?* I wondered. *Did this man just provide clarity on an issue that's been bothering me for months?* This stranger actually knew some of the same people I knew! He affirmed their character. He confirmed the project's impact. And it all happened in Millinocket, of all places. What do you think of that? For me, the scenario reminded me once again that God sees me, He hears me, and He cares for me. And He will meet me wherever I am. Even in the middle of nowhere. And He'll do that for you too.

The last miraculous experience occurred on the last day of my trip. Can you imagine what it involved? You guessed it — the minivan! I had maintained a thankful attitude for my vacation van. But I still questioned its purpose. *Is there some reason I have this car?* I wondered. You may think my quest to find deeper meaning behind everything is silly. Or maybe you relate? I admit the way my mind works is interesting sometimes.

On the last night of our trip, Andrew and I ventured south. He voiced his desire to visit the ocean, and I agreed to his request. My dear college friend, Laurel Libby, lives in southern Maine. We stayed with her for our last night. Her home offered easy access to the ocean. Laurel informed me ahead of time that she wouldn't be able to visit with me. At that present moment, her work demanded every hour of her attention. True to her word, Laurel arrived home after we went to bed, and she left the next morning shortly after I awoke. I thanked Laurel for allowing us to stay and assured her I understood her situation. Even though I wasn't able to visit with my friend, Andrew and I thoroughly enjoyed her four children. They are similar in age to my children, and delightful! Andrew has never met a stranger and eagerly jumped into playtime.

As I figured out plans for the beach, I heard a gentle whisper in my ear, *"Elizabeth, consider taking ALL of the kids with you to the beach. This is why you have the van."* The words dropped into my heart with such suddenness, I felt certain the prompting was from the Holy Spirit. Another phrase soon followed. *"The world, with one small exception, is composed of others."* It's my favorite phrase from John Maxwell, world-renowned leadership expert.

My heart leaped for joy! Of course — there *was* a greater plan for the van!

I cleared the idea with my friend. She consented, and I presented the idea to the kids. They were elated! "We live close to the ocean, but we don't go very often," Laurel's oldest daughter informed me. We loaded the van to capacity and traveled to the beach for a morning of fun. My heart felt so full as I realized once again that God's plans were so much bigger than my ideas. I could just imagine Him grinning as the purposeful puzzle pieces for the van fit together.

The entire adventure reminded me to look for the miraculous within the mundane. Because those moments do happen. My van example may seem simple and almost silly. However, as I close out this book, would you consider asking yourself the following questions: Are you created to live in community? Can serving lead to satisfaction? Do your decisions affect others' destinies? Does God value you and can He speak to you no matter where you are? I think the answer to all of these questions is a resounding, "Yes!"

In our lives there will be times when we stand at a crossroads, wondering what decisions to make and which direction to go. When I started writing this book, I felt that way. Confusion constricted my creativity. Darkness shrouded my dreams. Busyness burdened my being. Needless to say, I no longer feel quite so conflicted about my direction or my purpose. My Millinocket memories renewed my perspective and generated gratitude. As I reflected on the relationships and stories from my past, I discovered that life is actually much simpler than I often make it. I think my purpose — and yours — can be summed up in eight simple words: love God, love people; serve God, serve people. A couple I admire uses this phrase as the mission statement for their family. I think I'll start using it, too.

I often question, "Is life truly that simple?" I'm beginning to think it is. Maybe my incessant thinking complicates things that are quite straightforward! Have you ever been guilty of doing that? My vision for the future is simpler now. I have peace about my purpose. I am once again committing my way to God. How about you? I believe He'll keep my path straight. I believe He'll do that for you too.

I recently finished reading a beautiful book called *Teatime Discipleship*. Author Sally Clarkson shares stories and thoughts about connecting with the community around us, pursuing lives of purpose and faith, and enjoying the simple moments we encounter every day. She wraps up her book with an encouraging word.

"God did not make us to be slaves of works, and God didn't make us to use us — He is complete. God wanted sons and daughters to love, communicate with, and engage with...He created a gorgeous world to enjoy, food to feast on, experiences to enjoy."

Isn't that beautiful?

Can I remind you to rest despite the rush, to breathe despite your burdens, and to laugh despite the long road ahead? I believe it will all be worth it.

As I come to the end of this road, I want to thank you for joining me on this journey. It's been a joy sharing these memories with you! I also want to encourage you to continue walking within your own story, living each day by beautiful day with thankfulness, grateful for the people, places, and projects found within your path.

ACKNOWLEDGMENTS

W hen I think about all the people and pieces that fit together to bring this book to life, I am overcome with gratitude. Where do I even begin?

I must begin by thanking my Lord and Savior, Jesus Christ. He's the true author of my story, and I give Him all the glory and praise for this project. He ever so gently led me through this journey and followed me with His goodness and grace. Thank you, Jesus.

Next, I have so many people who supported me along the way. Starting with my husband, Isaac, thank you for challenging me to "Just do it!" If not for your comment, I might have continued to hesitate! And thank you for designing the book cover and layout. Your creative talents are amazing!

To my kids - Andrew, Charis, Wyatt, and Liam - thank you for your patience as I spent many weekends removed from family time, working on this book! You are the joy of my life, and I love you more than words can express.

I also want to thank my Reed family. You believed in me from the start! You read each chapter with excitement and filled in my memory gaps when needed. It's been great to re-live our Maine adventures together!

Next, there's everyone who collaborated to complete this book. To my dear friend, Katelyn Swiatek, thank you for speaking life into me through each step of this past year! You are a true friend who encourages me to become better in every way. I especially want to thank you for connecting me with my editor, Teri Nott.

To my editor, Teri, you are a joy! Your communication skills are brilliant! You insightfully helped identify my audience and unified the message of the book! You also patiently coached me in writing and taught me so much. Not only do I value your professional abilities, but I now treasure you as a friend.

To my friend, Sara Wasser, thank you for introducing me to Stephanie Pierucci and Pierucci Publishing! I am so grateful for your strategic mind! To Stephanie and the Pierucci Publishing team, your energy and vision are incredible! You immediately undergirded me and empowered me to release this book quickly! What normally takes months to complete, you finished in weeks. Thank you for pushing the boundaries on the timeline and proving that anything is possible to those who believe!

To all my advanced readers - thank you for taking your time to pre-read the book and give your reviews. Your support means more to me than I can adequately express.

Lastly, I want to thank every other friend who supported me throughout this project. There are so many of you, so I won't list all of your names for hesitation that I will miss someone. Some of you read rough drafts and shared your feedback. Others watched my kids while I wrote. Many prayed for me as I navigated this season. And then there was my dear friend, Evelyn Rennich, who did all of the above. I couldn't have made this journey without each and every one of you. I dearly love you all.

CONNECT WITH ELIZABETH

elizabethreedwatkins.com

Facebook

www.ingramcontent.com/pod-product-compliance
Lightning Source LLC
Chambersburg PA
CBHW061143120626
46546CB00005B/1904